Praise for

"I have personally been involved with Genevieve's journey with Pajama Program since its early days. She left her comfortable career to take a chance on a voice from her heart that deeply challenged the life she thought she wanted. Genevieve is an inspiration to anyone who ever felt trapped in a job or life. She's an example of how to take the leap that will fill your life with purpose and help you to be the person you really want to be."

—Meredith Vieira, broadcast journalist and television host

"Genevieve's decision to dramatically alter her career path after nearly 20 years was a leap of faith that has taught her about trusting yourself and living a life you believe in. She has met challenges every step of the way and is open and eager to share all the lessons she's learned. As an author myself, I understand what it takes to translate your heartfelt purpose onto the pages of a book. I found my purpose as a chef, and I know Genevieve found her purpose in pajamas! Now she pours her heart out in the hopes of helping others find *their* pajamas!"

—Carla Hall, chef, author, TV host

"The beautiful and inspiring journey of Genevieve Piturro reinforces the true meaning of purpose, passion, and relentless determination. It reminds us all how the power of ONE and human connections can change lives."

—Laura Schroff, #1 *New York Times* and internationally bestselling author of *An Invisible Thread*

"Genevieve has inspired thousands of Carter's employees and our customers to join in her mission to ensure that millions of children in need know that they are loved."

—Michael D. Casey, chairman and chief executive officer, Carter's, Inc.

GENEVIEVE M. PITURRO

FOUNDER OF PAJAMA PROGRAM

Purpose
Passion
and Pajamas

How to Transform Your Life,
Embrace the Human Connection,
and Lead With Meaning

RIVER GROVE
BOOKS

Published by River Grove Books
Austin, TX
www.rivergrovebooks.com

Distributed by River Grove Books

Design and composition by Greenleaf Book Group
Cover design by Greenleaf Book Group
Sketch of little girl, "Hope," credit: Nicole Caggiano
Cover pajama photo credit: www.FrankRiversPhotography.com
Photograph on page vi courtesy of Harpo, Inc./George Burns.

Publisher's Cataloging-in-Publication data is available.

Print ISBN: 978-1-63299-290-1

eBook ISBN: 978-1-63299-291-8

First Edition

This book is dedicated to the children on our wait list.
Pajamas are coming your way, I promise.

And to all those who know deep in their hearts
it's *not about the pajamas.*

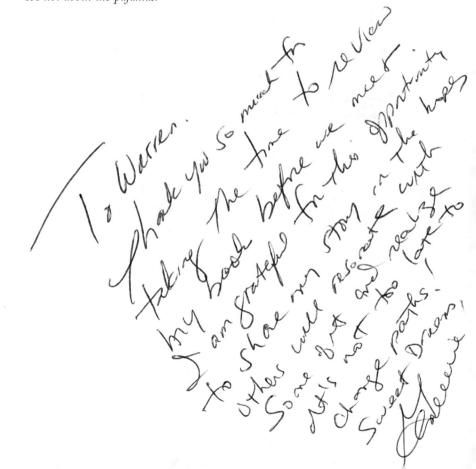

When I was invited to be a guest on Oprah, I didn't sleep for weeks. And the surprise
by Oprah and her audience that day was better than any dream!

Photograph courtesy of Harpo, Inc./George Burns

Contents

Author's Note

As my book was being prepared for publication, the international COVID-19 pandemic and quarantine struck all of us. My mom was diagnosed with COVID-19 and I was petrified. I thank God she recovered. My prayers are with all of you and your loved ones whose health has been at risk. To those who have been on the front lines of this virus and its repercussions, you have my profound gratitude for working so hard and so long to shield the rest of us from danger.

We have all been consumed with coping in our new reality. In this incredibly unsettling time when so many of us are worried and fearful about what comes next, I am continually inspired, and so often overcome, by what I see every single day through our human connection. From day one, people around the world have been there for each other, bringing light to dark days. We've seen window visits to the elderly, music serenades from balconies, car parades for "COVID birthdays," and teachers doing drive-bys to encourage their students; even celebrities calling bingo for nursing home residents. We're all reaching out, making calls, dropping off packages, carrying family and friends who've needed a lift, and standing with strangers where loved ones weren't allowed. And when we need a hand ourselves, we ask for one and it is given.

We are all finally *really* listening to one another, and we see each other more clearly. We are focusing on finding meaning and purpose in our lives, leading with our hearts, owning authenticity, and recognizing hope in our neighbors' eyes.

So here we are—stepping up, opening up, and looking up. The reality of getting back to work is emerging too, as offices and team interactions will most certainly look and feel different in the future. Lesley Jane Seymour of CoveyClub said something recently about future leaders that resonated with me: "We are at this moment of great re-invention, and it's a wake-up call for everybody. We're looking for a more compassionate, kinder, gentler, lead-by-example leadership style."

Today, we stand on the precipice of a new normal, personally and professionally. As we hope the light at the end of the COVID-19 tunnel remains bright, we must turn our hearts to another healing, and that is to eradicate the racial injustices that have been too many for too long. Planning the next chapters of our lives now, we are re-evaluating our choices and finding dignified and just measures for inclusive, innovative, and empowering ways to come together. I find myself yearning for meaningful ways to make a difference and to contribute to the beauty I see in people and our world. And I believe you want that too.

One secret I learned during the 20 years of growing Pajama Program is that the power of one doesn't hold much weight. That's because it's really the power of one-ANOTHER that gets the job done. Our human connection has been revitalized and is propelling us forward in ways we have never before witnessed. We're starting to feel love, when previously there was fear.

My husband told me, "Fear freezes the heart, but passion melts the fear."

Let's go for the passion; let's go for the love.

Acknowledgments

I WILL NEVER be able to express my deepest love and affection to Pajama Program's past and present board of directors, staff, chapter presidents, volunteers, and supporters. You all felt that frightened little girl's loneliness just like I did, so you wrapped your hearts around a little idea and gave it wings. Every day you are committed to showing our children tenderness and compassion, making sure they feel loved and comforted every night. I am forever grateful to you.

Thank you . . .

To my mom, who gave me such a loving bedtime filled with kisses and hugs and laughter. You knew the true meaning of "tucking me in" and you inspired me to make a difference for these children.

To my dad, who encouraged me to do my best and never give up.

To my husband, Demo, who taught me to dream boldly, listen to my heart, believe in myself, trust the universe, and expect miracles. You knew it was all possible.

To my sister, Patrice, who, next to our mom, is the best mother I know.

To my brother Frank, for building Pajama Program our first home.

To my brother Laurence, for always making me laugh at myself, especially on the days I needed a lift.

To Danny, Daniel, Joey, Michael, Rebecca, Christopher, and Mason, who fill my heart with sheer joy and unconditional love every day. You helped me to remember how precious childhood is.

To Nicole, who drew Hope so we would never lose her.

To photographer and friend Frank R. for always saying yes.

To the talented editors who helped me through this process, and especially my Greenleaf team. I didn't know how to write a book, and I have treasured your crystal clear direction and earnest support through every page.

To my family and friends, who understand that when your heart whispers, you listen. Please keep connecting. It's the most purposeful part of living.

There Is Enough

*H*er big brown eyes were locked on the pretty pink pajamas I held out to her, but she hesitated to take them.

"Don't you want these?" I gently asked.

She glanced from the pink flannel to the other children who held their new nightwear. At this shelter and after-school program in New York City, there were about 12 children in all, many here because of abusive or absent fathers, or mothers who were battered or headed for drug rehab—or prison. The girl looked cautiously at me kneeling in front of her, ridiculously overdressed in my corporate pantsuit. She turned to watch the other children head to the back room with their garments.

Then she looked at me again.

"What are they?" she whispered.

"They're pajamas," I said.

"Where do I wear them?"

"To bed at night."

She shook her head, puzzled.

"What do you usually wear to sleep?" I asked.

"My pants," she said softly, tugging on her too-tight, too-short, dirty pants.

I tried to make sense of what she'd just said. My mind was racing. Surely I'd heard her wrong. I needed a minute to rewind our conversation, to put it right in my mind. And I needed to keep from crying before she thought she'd done something wrong. My brain scrambled to steady itself and respond in a way that didn't show her how shaken I was, how upside down everything had become.

"Well, now you don't have to wear your pants to bed," I said. "Tonight you can wear these soft, pretty pajamas."

Her face registered little emotion as she tentatively accepted the gift. A staff member and I found a private place where she could change. In what seemed like slow motion, we watched as the most precious smile appeared on her face, and a tiny giggle escaped. The staffer took her hand and led her into the other room to sleep. Then my tears came. And I let them.

I didn't know it then, but it was in that moment, the most poignant I've ever experienced, that Pajama Program was born.

With that little girl, I found my true purpose in life, a purpose that would propel me day and night. It was also then that I realized there is enough in this world—more than enough, in fact—to fix situations like this.

There's plenty of food around, but somehow not enough for everyone. Many of us live in houses, but others live on the streets because they have nowhere to call home. Most people have winter coats to wear when it's cold, but we see men and women huddled under dirty rags and plastic bags to stay warm. We wish for every child to have a mom or dad to tuck them into bed at night and be there in the morning for breakfast . . . and yet they don't.

———

LIKE MOST OF us, I saw so much lacking for so many people. But in that moment at the shelter, something switched on in my brain. I thought: *There is enough. We're just all brainwashed to accept that there isn't. But if we share, come together, and look out for one another when we see a need, we will find that there is more than enough of what can really change things—compassion, integrity, love. I realized it wasn't the universe that was limited at all; it was us.*

Maybe it wasn't my brain telling me to see things differently. Maybe my heart just found its voice.

So, pajamas for these children it is. *It's a small thing, I thought . . . isn't it?*

Today, so many of us seem to be struggling with the same issue: We're living every day without meaning, feeling unsatisfied and disappointed. And sadly, everyone seems to be on the same page. Corporate leaders are struggling to keep their teams engaged and committed, and employees are going to work every day feeling unmotivated, disinterested in company goals, and apathetic about their jobs.

Why? I believe it's because the *human connection is disappearing right before our eyes.* The human connection is the key to thriving both personally and professionally. When we take the time to connect— I'm talking about face-to-face with our family, our partners, our friends, and our colleagues—our hearts feel fuller and, in fact, become healthier.

Scientists are investigating the biological and behavioral factors that account for the health benefits of connecting with others. For example, they've found that it helps relieve harmful levels of stress, which can adversely affect coronary arteries, gut function, insulin regulation, and the immune system. Another line of research suggests that caring behaviors trigger the release of stress-reducing hormones.[1]

When we restore the human connection to our lives, we also restore meaning to our lives because we start to care about each other and what we can accomplish together.

How do I know this? Because I was disconnected myself 20 years ago. It took a little girl's simple question to unnerve me and then propel me into a life filled with meaning. I am a witness to the power of the human connection at work.

I can tell you that if it happened for me, it can happen for you. This book is the story of how I found meaning and purpose in my life, and how you can, too.

---

1   "The health benefits of strong relationships," December 2010, https://www.health.
    harvard.edu/newsletter_article/the-health-benefits-of-strong-relationships.

Chapter 1

There's a Talking Peanut in My Candy Bar

I grew up in a large Italian-American family with more than enough love to go around. Money, on the other hand, was tight, and my mom and dad worked hard sticking to a budget that didn't leave much room for anything beyond the essentials. We were a group of six, and traditional, tasty Italian recipes with pasta and potatoes helped stretch resources.

My father, Frank, was an immigrant. He grew up in Matera, a poor, sleepy Italian village that is now a popular tourist destination famous for its Paleolithic cave dwellings. An only child, he came to the US at the age of 15 on a boat with his father. They were forced to leave his mother behind because she had influenza, which they were told would prohibit her from entering the US. She was devastated at the thought of being separated from her only child, but she vowed to join them later. And she did, one year later.

When my dad and grandfather showed up in New York City, neither of them spoke a word of English. They moved into my grandfather's sister's multilevel house in Yonkers. Each floor was home to a different part of their family. My grandfather was the last sibling to come over; he and my dad were taken care of by the rest of the family until my grandfather could find a job. He soon found work as a barber in Brooklyn, while my dad went to school and learned English. In college, my father studied civil engineering and eventually went to work for the New York City traffic department.

My mother, Marchita, grew up in Yonkers, the eldest of two girls. Her dad was born in Italy, and her mother, of Sicilian descent, was born in the US. My grandmother was a homemaker and a beautiful pianist. Everyone could hear her playing the piano when the door was open, and I've been told it was magical. My mom still has that piano today.

Mom worked for years as an executive secretary at McCann Erickson (now McCann), a global advertising agency in Manhattan. She loved everything about her glamorous job, including the Metro-North commute every morning and evening! My parents married when they were both 25. When my mother became pregnant with me, she quit her advertising job. Three more children soon followed.

Our home in Yonkers was a medium-sized, three-bedroom house. It was your average household in the 1960s and '70s, and we followed typical routines: school, homework, dinner, a little TV, then time to put on our pajamas, say our prayers, and get in bed so Mom could read us a story and tuck us in.

The importance of bedtime rituals

EVEN AS A child, I loved the coziness and comfort of bedtime. In addition to the many books she read us, my mom made up her own funny bedtime stories. To this day, one very special story brings tears to my eyes, filling me with so much love and gratitude for my mother who, even now, is the person I want when I can't sleep. The story is about a little boy eating a candy bar with peanuts when one peanut comes alive and shouts, "Don't eat me, don't eat me!" That always made us giggle and demand of our mother, "Tell us again, tell us again!"

All the laughing and hugging tired us out, and sleep quickly followed.

I was always conscious of our family's financial limitations, and it was obvious to me that most of my friends had more than I did. We had bag lunches and were rarely given money for hot lunches; we got new store-brand clothes, but only at the start of the school year and again at Easter, and the items were always on sale. But we had one thing in abundance—we had love.

As the oldest, I had a lot of responsibilities—including setting an example for my three siblings. Getting A-grades in school was of the utmost importance in our home. Luckily, I was a natural-born nerd, so I had no problem with this directive. I feared my father's wrath if I ever tried drinking alcohol, smoking cigarettes, staying out past curfew, or hanging out with the "bad kids." I hung out with the brainy crowd; there was no chance I would be invited into the "bad" club.

But I did insist on one thing, and that was freedom. I absolutely, PASSIONATELY hated confinement! I downright abhorred the feeling that someone or something was holding me back or limiting me in any way. My mom says even before I could walk, I managed to hoist myself over my crib bars and plop to the floor to "escape." Whenever I could taste and feel freedom, I reached for it every chance I got.

The main way I escaped feeling confined was through reading, which I did for hours at a time. I read book after book and wrote to almost every author to tell them what I thought. Some of them even wrote back. What anticipation I felt waiting for the mail every day, thrilled beyond belief whenever I received another handwritten response! I meticulously saved these letters in a three-ring binder, and I read them over and over, wondering what it might be like to write a book one day.

———

PART-TIME JOBS WERE expected of all of us kids. My first job (I think I was about 12) was sharing my brother's paper route, and I was in heaven. On collection day, when I was paid all in cash, I felt like I was a millionaire. I remember feeling so independent and knowing this was a very good thing. I was breaking out!

At 16, I landed a part-time job at a new B. Dalton bookstore, working evenings and weekends. I could hardly believe thousands of magical books were all around me, and I planned to read every one. Several of us were hired to get the store ready for business, and my coworker, Mary, and I became fast friends (and are still close to this day). We worked together, and then got fired together, right before opening day. We were only the pre-opening crew! We were crushed.

Together, we took ourselves to Alexander's department store up the street, got new jobs, and had a ball . . . and bought lots of cool clothes. I worked in the men's pants department (I got lots of jokes), and Mary worked in the sundries department. Mary also had a car, and that was the beginning of many more exciting days ahead for this nerdy teenager!

My parents definitely expected me to go to college, so I worked hard and was thrilled and proud to get into Fordham University. It was only a 15-minute drive away, but I really wanted to live on campus—I yearned for my independence. But my parents wouldn't allow it. I begged, cried, and threatened to move out against their will, but they were convinced living on my own would cast a cloud over them. They told me the family was a wheel, and a cog would be missing if I left. They were afraid of what their friends would say if their first-born was so desperate to leave the nest—which, in a way, I was. Finally, they went to see a priest about this dilemma, and we compromised: I could live sophomore year on campus, only if it was in the all-girls dorm with a roommate. *Hallelujah!* This was a rock-solid victory for my independence.

Eleven months later, I moved onto campus, signed up to write for the college newspaper, explored all the neighborhood hot spots, and started dating college guys. I got a stint at Fordham's radio station, WFUV-FM, as a DJ and host of a public affairs show, and that's where I found my voice, literally. I was having the time of my life.

As I began college, I swapped my sales job for a part-time job in a chiropractor's office. It seemed that all my money was spent on books and supplies, with just quarters left over for the gas tank of an old turquoise-colored Dodge Dart (I kid you not) that I shared with my brother.

I was always below that empty line when I rolled into the station, struggling to find quarters to fill up the tank enough to get me to my job or school, or back to my brother. But that colorful car had one charming result. On an unusually hot spring day, it puttered and slowed to a stop on the way to work. I got out and stood, sweating and looking at the car in a way that said, "I don't know what I'm looking for, but maybe the car will magically start again if I keep staring at it."

In the distance, I saw a jogger coming my way, and as he got closer, I thought, *Gee, he's pretty cute.* Cute he was, and he was also just what the mechanic ordered—a prince charming. He didn't have a white horse, but as it turned out he lived nearby and had a car to carry me off! He had my car towed and fixed, and we dated for three months. Then the car died for good.

College and that cantankerous old car proved invaluable preparation for my later professional life, which I continued to steer up the corporate ladder at all costs. I loved my job at WFUV and graduated with a degree in communications in 1983. I hustled, answering any ad that looked like it was for a radio- or TV-related position. One morning, I called WINS radio in New York and just started blabbering to the operator about how I had been on WFUV radio, and all I had done there, and that I wanted to speak with the station director. For some reason, she connected me, and he took the call.

I blabbered some more, and he kept asking me questions. Finally, he said he was starting a 24-hour news service called NEWSPHONE, and my phone voice was good enough for an audition. That's all it took for me to know I wanted that job. I got myself on the train the next day and applied. I ended up getting the midnight-to-8 a.m. shift sitting in a tiny room with a microphone and recording one-minute segments of the top news stories every hour. People could call in and hear the leading headlines 24 hours a day.

Unfortunately, nine months in at NEWSPHONE, the project folded—not enough people wanted to dial in to hear the news. Fortunately, the vice president of Group W Productions, the parent company, hired me for a position in the television syndication division, and I entered the world of television. I was a single, professional woman in a big city climbing the corporate TV ladder—I was Mary Tyler Moore!

———

THE WORLD OF television was thrilling, and after four years in the sales division I was ready to switch over to the creative side. I landed a job in marketing and worked long hours making a name for myself designing creative promotional materials for the shows syndicated by my employer, All American Television. I was often the first person in and the last to leave, but I didn't care. I had found my niche and wanted to climb that corporate ladder up, up, up. Two years in, I was promoted to manager, then director.

A few years later, as the vice president of creative services at D.L. Taffner Syndication Sales, I was convinced I had the best job ever. I was tasked with coordinating press interviews and promoting TV movies and shows as they entered into reruns across the US. In Los Angeles, I worked with the actor John Ritter on promos for reruns of *Three's Company*. I was meeting celebrities I had watched as a kid, and I loved every incredible moment!

"This is my dream job," I decided. "It can't get any better than this!"

I attended all the national and international TV conferences held in major cities in the US and in Cannes, France, and Monte Carlo, Monaco. I jetted to Rome, London, and Paris working on PR for the company's new made-for-TV movies. Life was good, and I was officially a workaholic.

I liked my job's glamour factor: I took limos, had an unlimited expense account to entertain clients, ate at amazing restaurants, and even sat in the skybox at Shea Stadium. My colleagues and I were living the dream—sitting on top of the world. (To this day we reminisce about how decadent those days and nights were, all in the name of doing good work!) It was a professional woman's fantasy come to life.

But that wasn't all.

By that time, I owned a one-bedroom co-op in the pretty and lush Riverdale area of the Bronx. If I wanted a big floral print on my bedding, curtains, and lampshades, I bought it. If I chose to stay at work until midnight to finish a press mailing, I did. If I wanted to visit a friend in LA for the weekend, I booked a ticket. I had built a world where it was all possible.

I dated (and loved) in those years, but my real true love was searching—traveling the world and looking for exciting experiences around every corner. My friends all had the marriage bug; one in particular had her baby clock ticking a mile a minute since the day she turned 21. I never did hear my clock tick, and I wondered if that was strange. But it didn't matter. In those years after college, I had my job, my apartment, and one very fabulous life. That was all I needed, or so I thought at age 25.

I had no idea how wrong I was.

The Heart of the Matter

THE REASON FOR sharing my story and providing these "The Heart of the Matter" takeaways is so you know you are not alone if you, too, find yourself searching for more. What I realized over these past 20 years is that the lessons I learned apply to leadership—to the leader you are in your personal life, and the leader you are, or will become, in the business world. Lead with meaning, and others will follow. If any of what I've learned helps you, gives you pause, or supports you through your own path of twists and turns, I am grateful to have written this book.

The Heart of the Matter is this:

* Learn from your childhood lessons.

LIFE TENDS TO come full circle. I see now it was the foundation of my mother's love and my parents' commitment to us—as well as the sacrifices we made—that helped me to see clearly when everything I thought I wanted was challenged.

That foundation drove me to find my true passion in pajamas. My mother's expressions of love helped me identify exactly what was missing in that little girl's life. And my father's insistence on education and hard work showed me how to provide not only for myself but also for others—helping me redefine what it means to be a "family."

* Examine the way you've "always" done things.

PARTLY BECAUSE OF my family's hard work and sacrifices, I sometimes felt I didn't have enough. As a result, I started out in my career by focusing too much on what I wanted in terms of wealth and material possessions—money, clothes, apartment, travel. Soon the polish wore off those pursuits, however, and I was left unfulfilled. I knew I needed a change.

* Don't let tradition hold you back from your true purpose.

WE WERE RAISED to work hard and respect our family, and I spent many years fulfilling the role of dutiful daughter in my traditional Italian family, which included having a successful career, well-appointed condo, and nice clothes. I had no idea I would need to let those markers of success go when I first stepped into that homeless shelter to read bedtime stories to children. But I did let them go, and that opened the way to being free to pursue new goals, ones that would give my life meaning.

Chapter 2

Your Heart-Voice
Is Calling

One morning, I had a couple of hours to myself in my apartment, and I was deciding how to spend the time. There was no mess to clean up, everything was in its perfectly appointed place, and I had plenty of time before I had to get ready for a lunch date. I looked around for my stack of books. And right then and there, with my life exactly the way I wanted it, something unknown made me pause, and I heard an inner voice ask, "If this is my life for the next 30 years, is it enough?"

This question came out of the blue for me. I heard it loud and clear as if another "me" inside me had asked me. And the voice wasn't in my head but arose from another place—my heart. This was not a question I had ever before pondered, nor was it a way I'd ever questioned myself. What I heard sounded like me but was most definitely "my alternate voice."

I had never had second thoughts about the path I had taken, and I honestly loved my life and everything I had worked so hard to achieve and have. The only explanation I can offer for my sudden inner questioning is that something deep inside me was starting to surface and, unbeknownst to me, was ready to challenge me and my entire dream life. So you can imagine how incredibly stunned I was when I heard "myself" whispering back, "No, I think I missed something."

My mind raced to one thing—not having a family of my own. My brother and sister had five children between them, and these nephews and one niece were a special part of my life. I always melted when I heard their little voices call, "Aunt Gennie!" (I still melt, though they are adult voices now.) I loved dropping to the floor and joining in their games. Together we were silly, loud, tireless, and free. The world felt perfect when I was with them. Even with all the joy I felt in those hours, however, I didn't feel a "ticking clock" of my own. My fondest memories of a maternal kind of experience came when was I was nine and my brother, Laurence, was born. I loved taking care of him, teaching him first how to walk and then chasing after him for hours in a park. But soon I was a teenager and decided I'd rather leave the job of raising him to our mom!

What I did feel, though, was a growing need to connect with more children. My first thought was to do this through some sort of volunteer work. I didn't know if that would fill the childless void I felt, but I figured my first step should be to explore it.

At the same time, I also needed to explore what was happening with a surprising new man in my life. Keeping up with the hectic work schedule I'd been thriving on left little time for a serious romantic relationship. Family, friends, and dates, yes; but an all-encompassing, whirlwind, turn-my-life-upside-down, soulmate situation? I wasn't sure it was even possible. And honestly, I didn't want anything to thwart my climb up the corporate ladder.

However, the universe seemed to have another plan. Sometimes when you need something—or someone—*he finds you.*

———

SEVERAL YEARS AFTER I purchased my co-op in Riverdale, Demo rented an apartment on a higher floor in the same building. He had decided life in Manhattan was getting too cramped for his liking, so he moved 10 miles north to Riverdale, where he could see grass and trees as opposed to yet another skyscraper. I hadn't noticed Demo until I found myself running into him every other day—around our complex, on our commuter van, on the walk behind our building, and at the gym almost every time I worked out.

One day he was sitting next to me on the Metro-North shuttle, and the next we were both in line together at our local café. He even found a glove I didn't know I had dropped on the train and handed it to me as we exited our stop. Honestly, I thought these were all just coincidences and gave him only familiar nods.

Finally, several weeks into our chance meetings, he broke the silence between us with a question I found a little humorous: "You look like you have a tan. Have you been away?"

"A tan?" I laughed. "I don't have a tan. I've been in Ireland, where it rained every day!" We chuckled and went our separate ways.

The next time we bumped into each other was when I found myself behind him as he took a gulp from a water fountain at our building's swimming pool. When he stood and met my eyes, we connected in a "take your breath away" moment. He warmly extended his hand and formally introduced himself. "Hi, I'm

Demo DiMartile." *Hmmm,* I thought to myself . . . *an actual gentle-man.* I was smitten.

He asked me if I'd like to take a walk, and that's when he came clean. He said the first time I'd whisked by him two months earlier, his inner voice said loud and clear, "That's the woman I'm going to marry." He set out to learn my routine with the help of accomplices—including our doormen, who were clearly romantics; a motherly concierge, who monitored my comings and goings; the shuttle driver, who knew my train schedule; and the gym security team and swimming pool lifeguards, who knew I loved to work out and then swim first thing in the morning. With their help, he could run into me any time he wanted to—and he did!

In a few short months, Demo turned out to be "the one" for me, too. Little did I know then how deeply connected we were and how much he would help me along the twists and turns that lay ahead of me. Demo had studied acting at Boston University and moved to New York City after college. He'd been on Broadway and television, in music videos with the singer Sade, and in tons of commercials. But few people possess Demo's defining virtue, his deep spirituality. Demo teaches and produces guided healing meditations. He's insightful and incredibly perceptive, and he can connect to most people on a soul level. I've always been more of a no-nonsense, get-it-done, facts-on-paper kind of girl. His spiritual depths were a perfect yin to my practical yang.

In spite of my most valiant efforts to remain single, I married Demo when I was 38. He didn't have children, and as this was a first marriage for both of us, we thought we were free and clear of major struggles or challenges. *Ha!*

I knew I had to share my growing discontent about my career with my new husband. I knew he would understand. But I wasn't prepared for his instantaneous response: "Go for it. Find what you're looking for and don't stop until you find it."

At that point, I had done some charitable work with an organization I loved called Starlight Children's Foundation, which grants wishes to seriously ill children in the US, but that was the extent of my volunteering since the time I was a Girl Scout. I told Demo I'd love to volunteer with children. I knew there were shelters where abandoned children were taken for safety, and I asked some friends, colleagues, and even local police stations for any information they might have. It seemed like such a simple idea: help others, feel better, get back into rhythm with myself, maybe find my true purpose.

But that moment, the one simple moment when a little girl asked me what pajamas were—well, that was the defining moment that changed my entire life.

———

SINCE I LOVE to read, my first thought was that I could bring books and read to children who were in shelters at night. Demo was right there to encourage me. It was his gentle but insistent push that convinced me to get on the subway to a shelter that first time. I thought that maybe telling children bedtime stories would help to fill their needs and mine.

I didn't know where to call, so I started asking around, and someone suggested contacting police stations in New York City. Somehow, at some point, I had a phone number for a shelter on a piece of paper. I called and meekly asked, "Can I come in after work and read the children stories?"

"What a nice idea," said the woman who answered the phone. "Yes, that would be fine."

Mind you, this was before 9/11, when you could do something like that—call a shelter, ask to come in and volunteer, and be quickly welcomed. Nowadays, there is much more security for volunteers, and I doubt anyone just calls and asks the way I did. But I'd been given the go-ahead, so I bought a dozen children's storybooks and went in.

That week, I visited a shelter in Harlem for the first time. I finished work and took the train uptown. This part of town was totally unfamiliar to me, so I was a little nervous. I remember that it was getting dark, and there was an autumn chill in the air.

I reached the street where the shelter was located—a main thoroughfare dotted by a few bodegas. People were hustling in and out of buildings, and some men were huddled together smoking and talking. I found the address and opened a small glass door to find flickering fluorescent lights, chipped linoleum floors, and a rickety elevator. The woman on the phone had told me to go to the second floor.

Feeling very alone and out of my element, I was afraid to take the elevator, even though I quickly realized that being alone in a stairwell could have been just as problematic. I essentially ran up the two flights, checking over my shoulder every step of the way. I tried to calm myself down—I'd spend an hour reading, and we'd all have a good time, no big deal. I had a bag full of popular children's books, with colorful pictures.

A young woman dressed casually in jeans greeted me. I was more formal, in a corporate pantsuit, and I remember feeling so awkward, just ridiculously overdressed. I started to sense my own naïveté. The woman was all smiles and extremely grateful. She told me she had been a little surprised by my call.

"You brought them all these books?" she asked me, genuinely

touched. "Come, I'll get you settled in this room, then I'll bring the children in."

She led me into a room that was bare except for a few straight-backed chairs. It felt like an industrial workspace. The kids' coats were piled on a low shelf that ran along the walls.

Then I saw the children at the door. The anxiety left me immediately, and I exhaled a long breath. They walked into that near-empty room slowly, and I melted a little with every face I saw. I felt compelled to be upbeat and to give them a great evening, even though at that point, I had no idea how dire their circumstances were. I was so out of touch, so ignorant of their plight, and I was ashamed that I'd arrived thinking I could make this some sort of a "party."

That first night started off uncomfortably for all of us. I didn't know where to sit or stand, so I plopped myself down on the worn industrial carpet and the kids followed suit. I groped for a book that was just right and chose a story about an animal.

For the rest of the hour, I read . . . and read . . . and read. Like so many teachers do, I read a page and then showed them the accompanying picture in the book. Page by page, I watched their faces for reactions. I saw a few smiles and some curiosity, along with a lot of empty stares. I could feel some of the uneasiness in the room start to diminish as the evening went on and the kids got into the stories. A couple of them stretched out on the floor and seemed to breathe easier. Some of the children looked engaged in my stories; others just stared at me or the floor or looked around the room as if searching for something.

Nobody spoke—not any of the adults, and none of the children. I believed then and now that the kids were trying to "be good" because they were uncertain of where they were, why they were there, and what would happen next.

The last few minutes with the children were almost relaxed. I had a glimmer of hope that I was doing some good. I knew it wasn't a bedtime story the way I'd had when I was a kid, but I also knew instinctively that in terms of being read to, this was as good as it was going to get for these kids that night. I wasn't their mother—I was only a nice lady who stopped by to read them a story for an hour. A lady who might never be back.

As for me, our time together on the floor was the most still I had been in years. I was grounded and in touch with the combined souls of these kids and my own soul all at once. I felt connected to them somehow; it was as if the world had stopped, as if we were all headed somewhere new and safe together. Something in their faces had such a profound effect on me—their wide-eyed eagerness, maybe, or the whole novelty of the experience. The feelings of peace and protectiveness I shared with my nephews and niece sitting together on the floor was what brought me instinctively to the floor with these children.

I had no idea what the future would bring, but that night I felt a fullness in my heart where it had been empty before. Just as I felt compelled to sit on the floor in that room, simultaneously I was being pulled away from my life as I knew it. It was a totally unexpected, heaven-sent tipping point.

I'd just wanted to get in and out safely, spend an hour. That's it. Now I knew that wouldn't possibly be enough. I wanted to come back, and I wanted to find more places like this one.

Over the next several weeks, I visited and read with different groups in the New York City area. I quickly realized the emotional impact these children had on me. I was drawn to them in a protective way, and my need to comfort them felt overwhelming. There was something just so *right* about it all. Every time I had to leave, I had a difficult time finding the right words to say goodbye to the children. I hated these last moments because I felt I was leaving them alone and afraid. I knew most, if not all, of them would be gone the next time I came, and a new set of abandoned or abused children would be listening to me. The prospect was deeply upsetting.

I made sure my goodnights were cheerful and warm. I couldn't let my sad feelings show after filling their heads with so many happy endings. Still, I felt like a fraud, pretending tomorrow might be full of sunshine and happiness when I knew I couldn't deliver either.

As affecting as these experiences were for me, I grew restless. I couldn't stop thinking that maybe I could do more than simply read. I felt guilty walking out after an hour, leaving them with only books and a memory of story time. How much was I really helping? Was it more unsettling to them that I left them, too? Books had always been an escape for me as a child, but the discontentment that made me reach for a book was nothing compared to what these children were hoping to escape.

Was I fooling myself thinking I was doing something that made a difference? I continued my visits, reading to the children in a circle on the floor, and looking for a way to do more. Surely I'd find it.

———

ONE NIGHT, I followed a staffer who walked the children to the room where they would go to sleep. I peered in as the children were helped up onto futons and couches. They looked so dejected and weary. They didn't change clothes from what they had been wearing all day, or longer, and some were crying while a few huddled together. There were no reassuring words or comforting bedtime moments from a parent. The staff was helpful and kind, but they didn't make a fuss. Perhaps because the whole experience of being in a shelter was traumatic for the kids, the staffers wanted to keep things low-key.

A rush of memories flooded back to me from when my mom would put the four of us to bed. Bedtime was full of carefree, fun, warm, and cuddly moments. I felt loved. No worries, no concerns, no fears at all. What I was watching now was *not* the tender scene I remembered as a kid, and not the bedtime these kids should have, either.

Where are their pajamas? I thought to myself. I don't know why that was the first thought I had, but it was. I thought pajamas would make it better for the children. They should be comfortable, in soft PJs that fit them and wrapped them in love and coziness. For all the reasons parents and grandparents the world over put kids in pajamas at bedtime, I thought these children had a right to the same ritual. The phrase "put your pajamas on" conveys a million loving sentiments, and these children had a right to at least a few of those feelings, even if they came from a stranger.

On my way out the door of the shelter that night, I turned to one of the women. I didn't want to say the wrong thing, but before I knew it, a few words clumsily fell out of my mouth as I asked her, "Do you think I could bring some pajamas for the children next week?"

Clearly surprised but without hesitation, she said warmly, "That would be lovely."

The next Saturday, I went to Kohl's. I headed to the children's department and combed through the endless racks of pajamas—flannel and footed PJs with funny frogs and pink hearts, Tinker Bell and princesses, Snoopy and superheroes—and forced myself to stick to basics: tops and bottoms in pink for girls and blue for boys. I chose nearly a dozen in every size, 3 to 12.

I carried the PJs one armload at a time to the cashier's desk, stacking them as fast as I could on the counter and struggling to hold up the towering pile. A very tall and annoyed woman was paying for an infant onesie. I began removing the hangers as she huffed and puffed and made sure my stuff didn't touch hers. I'm sure she was hoping to find one of those plastic green separator bars they have in food stores at checkout. Who could blame her? It wasn't my turn to check out, and I was definitely infringing on her space. It sounds like a scene from a sitcom, but it wasn't funny. I was sweating profusely in my coat and scarf while trying to avoid glares from other impatient shoppers who had the unfortunate luck of being behind me in line.

Yet not one person asked me anything, and I didn't offer any explanation. For the life of me, I don't know why I didn't simply say, "You see, there are children sleeping in shelters in their clothes and they need pajamas." I guess I wasn't ready to share. The cashier just did her job in silence, and I was grateful. I tried to carry the dozen or so bags outside. Halfway to the door, I nearly toppled over from the weight. A kind, elderly man made his way over to help me, and he carried a couple of the bags to my car. He didn't say a word, either.

When my volunteer day rolled around, I schlepped most of those stuffed shopping bags into New York City on the train to work in the morning and then after work down the subway steps to ride uptown to the shelter. When I arrived, the woman in charge was curious and asked, "What do you have in all those bags?"

I explained that I had pajamas, and I had gotten the green light the week before to hand them out to children after I read them a story. She smiled and welcomed me.

I settled myself on the floor as usual, and the kids came to sit with me as I read the half-dozen books I'd brought. The children had already eaten their dinner, and when I finished reading, I saw many sleepy faces. I noticed a few of the children eyeing my shopping bags, and I was eager to see how they would react to what would happen next.

I asked the children to line up in front of me and told them I had a special surprise. One by one, I handed each child a pair of pajamas I thought would fit. A staffer then escorted the child with their new pajamas into the other room to sleep. A little girl who had been halfway through the line now stood before me. I guessed she was five or six years old. She was wearing a soiled pink top with flowers along the neckline, pinkish-purple pants that were too tight and too short, and dirty sneakers that looked like they were five sizes too big for her. Her two pigtails were loose and lopsided. None of the children displayed emotion that night and most avoided eye contact with me, but I could *feel* this girl in front of me. I knew she was yearning for something.

When our eyes met, I felt like she was trying to connect. I saw her searching for something in my eyes that would give her comfort, some assurance that she was safe, that she wasn't going to be there much longer, that how she was living wasn't real, that she could trust me to change it all. Maybe she hoped I would scoop her up and carry her away to a nice place and take care of her. It took me a few seconds to repeat the words I had said to the others who came before her.

"Honey, these pajamas are for you."

She looked at me, said nothing, and simply shook her head.

I persisted, gently. "I bet they'll fit you. And they're pink, just like your top."

Again, the same response. Not a word, just a slow shake of her head, no.

One of the shelter staffers came over to walk the little girl to the other room, but she resisted, making it known without words that she wanted to stand to the side and watch me hand out pajamas to the rest of the children. So, together, they watched me.

When the last child received his pajamas, I walked over to the little girl and tried again. I knelt down, held out the same pink set I had thrown over my shoulder, and brushed the sleeve of the pajamas across her hand.

"Feel how soft they are? They'll be so comfy to sleep in. I think you'll love them."

She looked at me and in a hushed voice asked, "What are they? What are paj . . ." Her voice trailed off as she struggled to say the word.

"They're pajamas," I said, confused.

"Where do I wear them?"

"To bed at night."

She shook her head, puzzled.

"What do you usually wear to sleep?" I asked.

"My pants," she said softly.

I struggled to stop the tears so she wouldn't think she said or did something wrong. She gently took the pajamas from me. I wanted to pull her close and give her a big hug (and run out the door with her, but I resisted, remembering one of the restrictions placed on volunteers there: no physical contact with the children). I gave her a big smile as the kind staffer walked the girl to the "bedroom," and then I had a good cry for myself. I felt like a fool and solemnly left the building.

———

PAJAMAS, JUST A simple thing. But I wanted the children to have something new—something clean and warm to sleep in—in a world where they had so little. I wanted them to have something of their very own, not hand-me-downs, used, torn, or dirty. Brand new, just for him or her, so the child would feel special. These children were already cheated out of so much that I didn't want them to be cheated out of pajamas, too.

I never asked questions about the children when I went to read. I watched and listened, but I didn't pry. That was partly because the staff wasn't giving me personal details, but I think it was also because I might not have been able to bear what they would say. I read the newspapers and watched the TV reports. I knew what horrible things adults did to kids, even their own kids. Up until then, when I'd seen things in the media, it had somehow seemed part of a different world. But this was personal to me now. I was connected to these children, even though I saw them only once. I was connected to their situations, to their lives, and to their nights.

I couldn't change what had brought those kids to that shelter in the first place. I did have control, however, over what I could do as a strong, capable woman. I could give them each a pair of pajamas. At least I could do that.

———

ONE COLD NIGHT, I was on my way to a shelter on the east side of Manhattan. It was dark, and I was walking through a desolate park carrying several heavy bags of pajamas and books. I never gave much thought to my safety. New York City always seemed like a very safe place to me—but at that moment, I realized I was alone and defenseless.

I sped up a bit. The front door of the shelter was about 150 feet in front of me when, all of a sudden, I heard a woman screaming at the top of her lungs. My heart pounding, I frantically looked to see where the noise was coming from. I saw a woman—short, stout, no coat or hat—running toward someone headed for the door of the shelter.

"NO NO NO NO, PLEASE, I'M SORRY, I'M SORRY!!" she shouted. She appeared to be chasing a man who was holding a child and running ahead of her. She kept screaming, "YOU CAN'T TAKE HER, SHE'S MY CHILD, SHE'S MINE! PLEASE, NOOOOOOOO!!!"

Horrified, I tried to piece the chaos together as best I could. The man was a police officer, and he had a little girl in his arms, maybe two years old, who was screaming and inconsolable. She wasn't speaking any real words, just crying hysterically. The officer was in a race, desperately trying to get into the shelter with the child before the woman could reach them. In a split second, the officer and child were inside where another woman was waiting, then he pulled the door closed and bolted it as fast as he could. The sobbing woman, presumably the child's mother, slammed into the door on the outside. She pounded and pounded and continued screaming, "OPEN THE DOOR!" But no one did.

The policeman and child disappeared, and I stood, silent in the cold, watching the mother pounding on the door. Finally, after a minute, she slid to the sidewalk crying, lost, and alone.

It was eerily quiet. There was no one else around. I stayed back, hidden in the park, weighed down with my heavy bags and my dark thoughts. What could this woman have done to lose her baby like this? The policeman had no clothes for the baby, no bag, nothing; he was obviously afraid for the child, and the child was absolutely petrified.

I was utterly frozen in fear and horror. This mother was traumatized. What was her crime? Was the policeman justified? Was I so completely oblivious to their world thinking there must be some explanation for this misunderstanding? I truly didn't know what to believe, but suddenly I saw myself from the outside. Here I was, a woman with dozens of pretty pajamas at home all neatly folded in deep drawers lined with scented paper. How could I have been so ignorant—believing my pajamas were making a difference in these children's lives? Did I truly believe that the only thing these children needed was to have a life more like mine? I felt ashamed; I needed to do some serious soul searching.

Every week, I met children whose lives were a mystery to me. I saw them cry, run and hide, stare at their shoes or gaze despondently into space, anything to avoid the pain of making eye contact with me. I always tried to find their eyes, but it clearly made them uncomfortable. I wondered why. Maybe because the people they trusted repeatedly abandoned them, punished them—or worse. It wasn't until years later that a director of a children's orphanage told me what horrible acts some children were forced to perform in exchange for a nice gift. Trust is in the eyes, and many of these children had been terribly betrayed.

On my visits, I saw them spend the entire hour while we were together scanning the room for a way out. I met mothers and grandmothers who were reticent to engage with me. I knew some of them desperately wanted their children back, and some of them didn't. But in those minutes watching that horrific scene at the door, I understood the looming danger that child faced from her own mother.

The staff at the shelter taught me a hard lesson about families in their world, about the cycle of violence, the devastating effects of drugs, and the paralyzing power of fear. These families were different from mine. Most weren't being separated from their children because they couldn't pay their rent; they were estranged because they posed a real physical danger to their children.

I tried to calm myself down. I knew I had to approach the shelter. The woman was weeping quietly, slumped at the base of the door. Another policeman appeared and came over to help her up. She was limp and silent, exhausted, and she let him direct her to his car. They drove away. There was no more screaming, just the ominous silence of defeat.

I pulled out my phone and nervously called my contact in the shelter. I was buzzed in, and then I ran as fast as I could up the stairs where I knew the children would be waiting. I tried to wipe the scene from my mind. I knew I couldn't ask questions; no one would answer them, anyway. I looked for the child who had just arrived, but I couldn't distinguish between one frightened face and another. Such profound sadness filled me. Slowly, I looked at the pajamas I brought and took inventory before I handed a staffer the bag. She told me there were more children in another room. I hoped I had enough gifts.

With a nod from her, I sat on the floor and opened a book. The children slowly sat next to me as she walked around giving them each their own pair of pajamas, and then helping them change as they listened to my words. It was a quiet night there, and now, all these years later, I try to remember if it was that quiet every night. Or was that night especially somber because the screams from outside had carried upstairs, silencing everyone?

For the first time, I saw what a shelter really was, who was brought there, and most importantly, how awful the circumstances of a child's arrival could be. This new understanding was now my reality. Knowing all this wasn't easy for me, but obviously having to live it, as the children did every day, was far worse. I wanted to give something to them for their difficult first nights. A pair of warm, snuggly new pajamas and a beautiful storybook filled with pictures would be my lullaby for these children in such pain tonight—until I considered what more I could do.

The Heart of the Matter

- Ask yourself, "If this is your life for the next 30 years, is it enough?"

THAT QUESTION CHANGED everything for me personally and professionally, because I knew it was my heart-voice speaking up. And it can do the same for you. If your answer to that question is no, explore it. Ask yourself what seems to be missing. Do you want more time for family, for friends, for leisure, for something you've put on the back burner? Do you need more time outdoors, or do you want more indoor solitude? What kinds of activities really get your heart-voice singing? For me, it turned out to be reading to children who had no one else who could do that for them. Once you start listening to your inner voice, you'll be amazed where it takes you.

- Never doubt that the smallest acts can trigger big changes in all aspects of your life, and the lives of others.

DON'T DISCOUNT THE value of any action you take or have experienced. It all adds up and presents itself in the end as a whole life. There are reasons why we feel what we feel and do what we do. Our memories and emotions hold the keys to our actions. Until

I met the little girl who changed everything for me, that talking peanut who cried, "Don't eat me!" in my mom's candy bar story remained buried deep in my childhood memory bank, a gentle reminder of those precious moments feeling loved as my mother tucked us into bed. It wasn't until that memory came to me 30 years later that I knew what I was witnessing was wrong and that I could help make a change, even a simple one.

- Embrace the human connection.

IN THE PAST 20 years, I have seen extraordinary things happen when people meet face-to-face. That's because it's here we begin to connect heart to heart. The human connection has inexplicable power. It can be profound and transforming, and it always evokes respect. It is in these moments when we lead with meaning, that we move mountains, and more significantly, it's when we move people.

In this book, you'll read about moments that have enlightened, comforted, and, in some cases, shocked me. The human connection is a theme that runs through most of them.

- Never doubt that the universe has your back.

LISTENING TO YOUR heart-voice and trusting yourself one step at a time summons the universe as your partner. Trying to get to the top of the corporate ladder took precedence over my personal life for many years. In fact, I was running so fast I didn't even notice how quickly time passed and how alone I was. When I began to slow down and listen to my heart instead of my head, I was directed to the answers I was looking for. Meeting a little girl in a shelter and Demo's appearance were just the start of the "universal encounters" that set me up for personal and professional transformation. There's no doubt in my mind that when we're on our true path, the stars align for us.

Chapter 3

Finding Your North Star in a Cloudy Sky

"I can't think of anything besides those children," I told Demo one night while putting on my own pajamas. "And when I get a call from a shelter, I can't get there fast enough."

"They're changing you," he said, with a nod.

He was right. My transformation had begun.

We all have our passions. Some people like to cook, others do 5K races every weekend, and some love to spend time outdoors enjoying nature. Regardless of what diverts them from their daily grind, people need outlets. Growing up, I had several hobbies that included playing the piano, stamp collecting, and writing letters to authors. Of course, the extent to which we invest ourselves in those outlets depends on our personalities. I'm one of those people who, when I'm in, I'm all in, obsessively. "Half-ass" has never been part of my vocabulary. But having hobbies to pass the time and feeling passionate about doing something are very different mindsets. When I saw the impact that a few pairs of pajamas could have on those children in need, I dove in, headfirst. In short measure, I became a woman possessed. The injustice of it all was gnawing at me, and I couldn't let it go.

About three months after I started bringing pajamas to children in shelters, I started receiving calls from caregivers throughout New York City telling me they'd heard from their friends about what I was doing. They wondered whether they could have some pajamas for the kids in their care, too. I heard some of their stories—some horrific, some just downright sad—about the children. Every single time I was asked for help, I said yes. These kids had already heard the word "no" too often in their lives.

I started to buy pajamas every chance I had. I made detours in my commute several times a week looking for sales. I combed the newspapers for closeouts, knowing my money would go farther if I could keep the prices down. I didn't need to pay for luxury pajamas, but I didn't want to skimp, either. These were very important pajamas going to some special VIPs. By this time, I'd racked up about $2,000 total in pajama buys. I'd made major purchases before—like furniture—which cost a lot more. Isn't this better? Yes, I answered myself. It's definitely better.

I was keeping a running total in my head of how many pajamas I was accumulating for boys versus girls. And then there were all the sizes. It was difficult to remember how many pajamas of each size I had at home, but rather than designing an efficient way to keep track, I overcompensated. *Cha-ching, cha-ching, cha-ching!*

At the time, my recording system was a green folder with NEEDS PAJAMAS handwritten on the front in thick black marker. It was filled with sheets of lined paper on which, also handwritten, I made three columns: the first for each shelter that called; the second for what they needed; and the third noting when I gave them pajamas. Many of those third columns remained empty, waiting for me to schedule a time to make deliveries. That green folder was becoming my most valued possession.

Most weekends, I drove for miles to strip malls, outlet stores, and going-out-of-business boutiques. After work and on my lunch hours, I took the subway throughout New York City—wherever I could find quantity and quality at a reasonable price. Taking a lunch hour was foreign to me, and I was beginning to feel like a criminal. Never before had I wanted to take a break during the day, I was so consumed with my career. But now things were different; now I was suddenly hungry.

I also made it a habit to ask everyone I knew to buy pajamas and bring them to me. Little did I know how those would pile up at my door. (They still do!) At night after dinner with Demo, I reached for my tape gun and boxed up the pajamas, writing out labels with my Sharpie until it ran out of ink and I ran out of steam. Most boxes were destined for lower Manhattan and Westchester, but some were now headed to New Jersey and Connecticut. I even added a new speed dial number to my phone—UPS, my faithful delivery service.

Suddenly, I had an amazing new sense of fulfillment in my life—I was happier than I'd been in years. But I was also torn and confused. As my pajama "passion" started to take over more and more of my life, I was running from town to town, with pajamas and books stuffed into our car trunk and piled high in the backseat, and I was starting to have quite a bit of trouble fulfilling all the endless promises I made on a daily basis. I knew I would have to learn to juggle better or make some major changes in my life.

I had always loved my job and my career, but this new love for the kids and pajamas was truly taking over my life. I was afraid, and I was getting no sleep. I couldn't leave the career I'd spent years building to focus on these children . . . could I? Demo believed in me and I drew incredible strength from his support, but I wanted a reality check, which wouldn't be easy.

How could I let my family and friends in on my secret thoughts when I didn't have clarity myself? I was afraid I would ramble on like an idiot, sinking any chance I might have of getting their support, let alone enthusiasm.

I'm rethinking my career . . . I haven't been feeling fulfilled . . . Something is missing in my life . . . I need to find my purpose . . . I think I found it giving a little girl pajamas.

Ugh. It sounded like I was reading too many self-help books on the way to a mental breakdown. All I could picture were people who thought I had good sense now looking at me like I had three heads, not one of which had a functioning brain.

No matter how I phrased it, it was all going to boil down to the only thing they would be able to hear: "I'm thinking of throwing away everything I've achieved in my career to walk around giving kids pajamas and books . . . And I have no idea how I will make enough money to eat."

Still, I couldn't shake the feeling that I needed some support and encouragement from the people who'd known me longest, who knew me best. Insecurity had me tied in knots. I was hiding my newfound hobby from my colleagues, thinking they'd surely laugh at me—or worse, shun me. If you told me a year previously I'd prefer to deliver pajamas to shelters over coming up with a winning marketing campaign, I would have said you didn't know me at all. Everyone knew I had my heart set on that impressive office with comfy chairs high in the sky, not on a bare room with makeshift beds.

But now I knew it was time to try out my pitch on a friend—not a close friend, but a friend unrelated to my career or family. This way I would be safe. She couldn't spread the word among my colleagues that I was contemplating jumping ship, and she didn't know anyone in my family so she couldn't let them know I was teetering on the edge of throwing everything away. I would try out my pitch on her and see her response.

I crafted what I thought were a few compassionate, thoughtful, and succinct sentences to let her know what I was thinking. One evening over drinks, I told her about my interest in doing some charity work, that I had thought it would be nice to spend time after work reading to children in shelters, how that led to handing out pajamas, and about the little girl who didn't even know what pajamas were. I skimmed over that story on purpose, though. I didn't want to take a chance on letting her in on my most private feelings. There was no way I'd let myself be that vulnerable and raw without knowing for certain I was in safe company.

I was nervous at first about telling her all this, but then I began hoping she'd be excited for me, maybe she'd want to help! If that happened, I'd let her in on everything about that evening with the little girl so she'd be as fired up as I was! I told her I was loving every minute of it, laughing off the large dent it was making in our household finances.

"I know it might seem sudden," I said, "but I'm ready to make a change. I honestly feel I've found my life purpose." I held my breath but tried hard to act indifferent and avoided eye contact as I sipped my red wine.

Her reaction? She took all of two seconds to say, "Why on earth would you drop your career for *that*?"

I was crushed. Deflated. Angry. Embarrassed. Her look was

anything but understanding, and I knew this conversation needed to end before I lost my temper or worse, melted into tears.

Every negative thought I had ever had, every single doubt, came crashing down on me. My heart was pounding, and I had to fight the urge to flee the table, to stalk out of the restaurant without a word. What *was* I thinking? Was this going to be everyone's reaction? Was I being stupid and naïve? Was I out of my mind? Should I stop all this nonsense now and chalk it up to a fairy-tale idea, something to think about if, and only if, I won the lottery? I was shaking on the inside and probably on the outside, too. But my friend didn't flinch, so I guess my acting was good.

"I was just thinking about it, that's all," I said nonchalantly.

All I remember after that is making an excuse for getting out of the dinner that was supposed to follow our cocktails. I was a hotbed of emotions. I was furious and annoyed that she didn't "get it." I was devastated that her first response wasn't "Wow, what a brilliant idea—count me in!" Instead, she smirked. I was heartbroken that she didn't immediately care about these children like I did. But mostly I was left confused and panicked about leaving my safety net and giving up everything for some crazy idea. What if my little pajama charity never gained traction? Then where would I be?

I kissed her goodbye, and our friendship began to fade away. I was distraught, but I remember Demo encouraging me. He told me, over and over, "It's your purpose. You cannot give up your purpose based on someone else's opinion. You have to trust *yourself*."

———

IT TOOK ME weeks before I tried telling someone again. While I was looking for honest feedback, even someone who might challenge my ideas so that I could think them through, I wasn't ready to be laughed at again. I was 38 years old and found myself having to regain my confidence, pull myself together, and approach my most formidable confidant, my father. He was a super-practical, business-oriented, and security-first man.

We sat down over a cup of coffee in his kitchen one day, and I told him my tentative plans. He reacted at first only slightly better than my friend did. I knew he was worried for me and genuinely concerned that I didn't really think this through, but he could tell I wanted, no, *needed* to be heard. So I talked, and he listened for a while that afternoon over coffee. He asked me tons of questions, and my palms began to sweat. (Was I applying for grants? Not yet. Did I have a business plan? Not really.) All the while, he gave me ideas to help me figure out how to make a living from this venture.

Finally, my father asked, "Will you be able to make enough of a difference for enough kids to make it all worthwhile?"

"I'll give it everything I have," I said. And he smiled.

By the end of our conversation, I knew I had a long way to go before my dreams became a reality, and he realized I was determined not to let this slip away. He listened some more, which helped restore a little bit of my confidence.

A few days later, I decided it was time to go to my North Star, my mother, and let her in on my secret thoughts. My parents had been divorced for some time by then, and I knew the conversation with my mother would be very different from the one I had with my father. After all, she is a mother, my amazing mother, who instinctively knew what pajamas, a story, and bedtime really meant: the cherished time when the bonds of love and security between parent and child cement the all-important foundation for a child's next day—and entire future. Was there ever a night when my mother, no matter how tired she was, or how many more chores she had left to do, failed to show up in my room at bedtime—ready to read, to listen, to let me know how special I was? None that I can recall.

My siblings and I reminisce about the times one of us felt sick during the night and all we had to do was whisper "Mom" softly and, in two seconds flat, we'd all hear her voice from her downstairs bedroom answer, "I'm coming." She was always there for us. Likewise, I have seen how bedtime in my sister Patrice's home has fostered that same unconditional love between her and her three boys. It's a revered ritual with profound significance, and my mother and Patrice, the two best moms I know, set the standard for me.

Just as I'd expected, my mother expressed little concern about any change of plans I might be mulling over. She didn't hesitate or take even a few minutes to mull over pros and cons. She thought it was a beautiful idea to find a way to help these children. She wasn't afraid for me, she trusted me, and just like that she shared her North Star power with me. A few encouraging words from those I trusted, admired, and leaned on reminded me that I was brave enough to make a leap and smart enough to navigate it. I began to trust myself on this strange new path. I was breathing again. One way or another, I would just have to learn how to juggle everything better.

But this truce was short-lived, as it quickly became clear that the two sides of my life—career and passion—were headed for a major head-on collision.

The Heart of the Matter

- Put your money where your heart-voice is.

WHEN YOU SPEND money, time, energy, and resources on something that brings you joy, the price will feel small compared to what you get in return. You'll realize the change you're making not only fulfills you, it contributes to the greater good. For me, the cost of not buying those pajamas would have been a far greater burden than my credit card debt.

- Reality checks are good—until they're not.

WHEN YOU'RE CONTEMPLATING a change, or a new path, whether it's personal or a different way of conducting business, you may seek out friends for support. But beware: You may run into some surprising negative reactions that stop you in your tracks. Do their objections make sense? Did they point out something you might want to fix before you proceed? What you do is your decision. You have to trust yourself.

- Be your own North Star.

JUST A FEW minutes of support from someone influential in your life can change your outlook and give you the courage and confidence to trust yourself and move forward. Reach out to someone you respect and admire, and share your dreams, challenges, and goals. Get their feedback and consider their ideas. And then move forward as your own North Star, lighting the way for yourself and others.

- Who or what is on your "needs pajamas" list?

YOU MAY FEEL passionate about the environment, animal welfare, politics, education, food security, or some other cause that "needs pajamas." Or perhaps you're not yet sure what you're passionate about and need to get involved in a variety of areas to see what rises to the top for you. Follow your gut. Just don't let uncertainty hold you back. Get out there, make some human connections, and start to live your life with more meaning.

Chapter 4

And Just Like That, the Raindrop Fell

At this point, I had been working in marketing for 18 years, and my experience in entertainment was opening doors for me to explore new opportunities in other areas. It was becoming increasingly clear, however, that I had little in common anymore with colleagues who were elevating their status in the business and expecting me to continue my climb.

Now that I knew the real meaning of life, I was looking for something different that could pay the bills. It was time to make a career-changing decision. I made the move from one company and a salaried job to marketing projects for a couple of companies. I wanted to manage my own time—that is to say, juggle it all with my beloved pajama endeavor.

I started to get to work early so I could get my pajama tasks finished first. Funny how "my career" changed to "the job." Marketing is many things, but the one thing it is not is constant. It has to be new and different, fresh and original, every single time. And of course, it most certainly has to be fabulous—all marketers are expected to be fabulous. I felt a constant pressure to be the best, to be brilliant for my bosses, when all I wanted to do was grab *Goodnight Moon* and read it to the new kids at the shelter.

Every day, I lugged to work all the things I planned to take care of—the bags of pajamas and storybooks that I had bought or that had been given to me, my tote full of packing materials and notes to put inside each box, everything I wanted to include in the cartons I was planning to send out that day. I hid all my papers in plastic tote bags I stapled and re-stapled shut in the coat closet, and I brought my rolling carry-on if I had pajamas to keep out of sight. Thankfully, that closet had plenty of room and no one asked questions. I kept track of my all-important "Needs Pajamas" list, which I compiled each night after making phone calls to shelters or fielding calls from them asking for pajamas.

I left nothing at any office. I carried it all with me on the trains every day. I remember one particular subway ride home when I was carrying a large and overstuffed plastic bag full of new pajamas I'd bought after work. I knew I was taking a chance, but I made it onto the crowded train car. I had to stand and hold on to a straphanger. The handle of my bag started to rip, and I closed my eyes and said a prayer. Just two more stops to Grand Central, I pleaded with the bag. I opened my eyes and saw a businessman making his way in my direction.

"Need a hand?" he asked.

"I need a suitcase," I answered. We both laughed. "My stop is next, so then I can get a seat on Metro-North."

Then he asked me a question that would soon become one I heard regularly: "Are you running a camp?"

I told this stranger the truth. "No, but I guess it looks like that. I was reading to children in a shelter and saw they were sleeping in their clothes, so now I bring pajamas for them whenever I can."

That was easy, and relatively painless, I thought. He looked at me expressionless but didn't say anything. I waited. He was searching for words, I could tell, but nothing came out. Maybe he was stunned that people actually did stuff like this, but I'll never know what he was thinking. The train door opened at my stop, and I headed to track 40.

I had to be cautious; I couldn't have any evidence of my other life anywhere in sight—it was almost like I was having an affair. To be honest, I thought I was brilliant. I was sure I was so adept at hiding my sneakiness that I would be able to manage all my lives seamlessly. And I was keeping it together—barely. Even Demo had no idea how much I was getting done for the children during the day. I didn't want him to know how big this thing was getting for fear that he would tell me to take it easy. "Slow down," he'd surely say. "Breathe . . . Do a little every day, and it will be enough until you figure out how to do it all."

I feigned calm and sanity on the outside, but on the inside it was a different story. I felt like my brain was screaming to go faster, do more, and get it all done. Pictures of these children and their sweet voices played over and over like a recording in my head. I kissed Demo goodbye every morning, took a deep breath, and let the race begin: show up at the office at dawn; return calls from shelters requesting pajamas; print out directions for driving to new locations; and respond to my pajama emails, which were tripling daily.

I would order PJs and books online, spending $500 to $600 every few weeks for up to 100 PJs and books. Then I would spend hours setting dates for my reading visits and for drop-offs to group homes and shelters. I also had to squeeze in meetings with people who had collected or purchased pajamas and books, not to mention find time to pack up the boxes I needed to send via UPS.

Working those early morning hours was the only way I could ensure none of my "real work" fell through the cracks. I could not afford to lose my jobs. When I had all my pajama bases covered, I got down to my paid work. I was sure I was successfully hiding my pajama trails, and no one was the wiser, but I couldn't hide the fact that when 6 p.m. rolled around and colleagues or friends wanted to go out for drinks, I was always too tired. Everyone knew that I was the first one in every day, everywhere, and thankfully my workaholic reputation was an easy excuse for all my yawning.

Though physically exhausted, I was mentally energized enough to spend the night awake, remembering something vital I had forgotten and planning the next day in even greater detail so as not to miss a beat. No matter how stressed I was or how busy, I was always ready for more in the morning.

I truly thought no one would notice that my attention to my "real" work was waning. *If I usually give 200% at work, I'm giving 100% now, so who can complain?* Looking back now, I guess this is how all people think when they lead a secret life. Until they get caught.

———

IN ONE OF my jobs, I was responsible for creating and organizing presentation materials to be sent to prospective clients, as well as going on the road to meet with present and future clients. My boss traveled so he did not come in every day, which was lucky for me. Between the days he was in meetings and the days he was out of town, I could pretty much get my personal work done along with everything I was doing at my job for him. I swear, I had it covered.

But on one particular day, I knew my boss was in the office, so I'd have to be even more discreet. I had my personal work hidden away and was busy prepping some marketing materials he had asked me to send out.

I was stuffing "sample kits" into boxes when I saw him approach. There were product items, descriptive brochures, photos, and a bunch of referral letters on my desk, all with my cover note on top. My eyes widened as I looked down and saw clearly for the first time what he was seeing as he came closer. My cover letter was not even centered on the stationery; it looked juvenile, atrocious even, but I had just been too preoccupied and rushed to bother redoing it like I told myself I would. I remember already being annoyed that day that he was in the office, as I had way too much to do to have to answer to him or have him watching me. All of that was taking time away from my all-consuming and much more important pajama work.

There he stood in front of me. He saw me practically throwing everything into a much-too-large box, leaving way too much room and ensuring everything would be tossed around before the client received it. I was attempting to tape the box closed and was making a complete mess of it. I mean, I knew the box was too big, and I knew my taping attempt looked like that of a four-year-old using a tape gun for the first time. By the time my boss got close enough to peer into the box, I couldn't bear to look at him. I saw the package in its entirety for the first time just the way he saw it—and that made me cringe. There was a terrifying silence. His baffled eyes found mine. Talk about a human connection.

"What are you doing? What are you doing??"

He was furious, and shocked. My face turned bright red, but I couldn't turn away and my mouth somehow didn't work. I had no defense. I was mortified, and all I wanted to do was hide. This was not me—I had always been an organized, eager-to-please, proud employee. Now I should have been committed to employee rehab. I stood before him, silent and frozen. He shook his head and walked away. I knew then everything had changed between us. The charade was over.

The truth is, I'm sure someone—maybe a potential client or a competitive co-worker—would have approached him soon enough to comment about my deteriorating skills. But even now, many years later, I can pull up that moment and that feeling of complete humiliation. I can still feel myself standing there, ashamed, with nothing to say for myself. I shudder at the memory. In the moments following that revelatory exchange, I knew there was no going back. There was no redeeming myself.

It was only a matter of time before I lost that job.

———

DEMO COULDN'T HELP but notice my growing frustrations with the business world. He sensed the deep significance I'd discovered in helping these children. He started talking to me now about seeking my life's true purpose, and he offered a quick tutorial in meditating to find it. "Ask the universe for help," he kept saying. "Just keep asking, and you'll be directed."

Demo has always had a clear perspective on the bigger picture of life. Along with his deeply spiritual side, he's a tried-and-true "stop and smell the roses" guy. I remember racing home one evening knowing Demo and I had a long to-do list for my project. I opened the door and there was my beloved, sitting on a stool in front of the picture window with an empty seat for me right beside him.

He turned to me and said, "Will you just look at this sunset? Let's watch together."

That's Demo in a nutshell. I move too fast to smell the roses. I trust the sun will rise and set; I don't have to watch it do so.

But as I sat there with my peaceful husband, my mind racing in a thousand directions, I wondered how someone like me was supposed to talk to the universe. And just what exactly was I supposed to be asking for?

Since I'd had that dreadful run-in with my boss at work, it seemed a good idea to seriously contemplate what it would take to make a major change in my life. There was just one problem, among the obvious other issues: Whenever I tried to get my head around actually making a plan of action, my thoughts, feelings, even my body seemed to go to war. My stomach would start churning. My throat would close up, making it hard to swallow. I felt confused and scared to death. Hundreds of emotions bombarded me. Even the words in my brain weren't connecting; it was as if my vocabulary had come unhinged.

I wanted desperately to put my feet firmly on the ground and know what I was doing. I am an orderly person and accustomed to moving in the direction I set for myself on any given project, so this feeling of being unorganized, incapable, and downright dizzy unnerved me. I worried I would expend so much energy without being focused that I wouldn't actually make a difference in the children's lives. It would end up being a waste: I would've done absolutely nothing to make a difference, certainly nothing I could be proud of.

Yes, I had given out hundreds of pajamas and books by now, but the stream of calls and requests that came in tripled by the week. The cat was out of the bag, so to speak, and shelter staffers shared my name and phone number with one another. Sneaking calls on my then-large cell phone got trickier by the minute. All I could see was what *I wasn't* doing, the children who hadn't gotten their pajamas yet, and the shelter staff people I would let down if I didn't find a better way.

I also had to face a solemn and sobering question: How could this work financially long-term? If I left my jobs and followed this new path, what would that mean to me—to us—financially? Demo was doing all he could to keep his commercial acting jobs coming, but in reality, more and more jobs were being filmed outside New York. He was worried about his work drying up, and now so was I. I wasn't much of a saver, and that unfortunate and short-sighted character flaw, in conjunction with Demo's on-again, off-again work-load, could lead very quickly to disaster.

While I stressed over possible financial ruin, something strange happened while I slept. I had started having dreams of being in cars, but never being in the driver's seat. I wasn't taking control of my own life. When I realized I had to "take the wheel," I knew things were going to change forever, and I knew I needed to ask Demo for some help beyond packing and delivering boxes. I also knew I'd discover a viable financial path in this new life ahead of us.

"You're always talking about the importance of knowing your life's purpose," I said one night as we got ready for bed. "You've taught me to follow my heart and believe I can find my true purpose and not just be a career woman. What do you think my life's purpose is? Please, tell me."

He answered my question, as anyone with true insight would have, with another question: "What do *you* think your purpose is?"

"I have no idea," I whined.

"Well, I have a pretty good idea," he responded. "But I want to be your husband, not your teacher. So I'll give you a simple exercise to do. That way, when you discover your purpose, it will have come from you, and it will empower you to trust yourself."

I was all ears.

"When you go to work on the train in the morning," he continued, "instead of filling your head with the newspaper and all the daily anxieties that overwhelm you, meditate. Try to still your mind, close your eyes, breathe deeply, and open your heart. Therein lies the purpose of your life and your courage to live it." He then repeated what he'd been saying for weeks: "Ask the universe for help. Say, 'I choose to have my life purpose revealed to me.' Then—and most importantly—just listen. You will be directed."

Meditate. Ask the universe. Huh. Who would've thought?

I took his advice. On the train at dawn, sitting at my office desk, walking through the city, putting sugar in my coffee, I repeated words to myself like "Please tell me what my purpose is. Please show me what I'm supposed to be doing. Is this what my life is supposed to be about? Pajamas and children's books?"

Nothing.

"Just keep asking," Demo insisted. "And keep *listening*."

Weeks went by. I meditated on my sofa, at my desk, in bed after my nighttime prayers.

Still nothing.

———

I WAS HEADED downtown one sunny afternoon for a work meeting when what felt like an invisible raindrop "plopped" onto the top of my head, and I heard the words "Pajama Program." It was subtle, yet definitely clear. It sounded like my voice but gentler and whisper-like, as if it came from far away.

Suddenly, I had an absolutely crystal-clear vision of those words on a sign, hanging above my head. The words "Pajama Program" were in soft, cloud-like lettering, similar to the bubble letters we used to write our names in grammar school. In my mind now, I was smiling, laughing, sitting with two or three children in my lap, and handing out pajamas, with a line of children in front of me that stretched for miles and miles.

It reminded me of a scene in *The Wizard of Oz*, one of my favorite movies to watch with my mom when I was little. In my mind's eye, all these smiling kids were lined up along the yellow brick road, waiting for their brightly colored pajamas. I laughed out loud at my vision, thinking it was surreal. But my heart was full—this was real. It wouldn't be just me, alone. If I set up the architecture, if I found friends to help, together we could help many, many children.

"Pajama Program." That was it!

I looked around at my fellow subway travelers, all of whom were in their own little worlds, preoccupied by their individual concerns and clearly oblivious to what I had felt and heard. It was nothing short of an epiphany. I mean, really, I'm telling you—it felt exactly like when you're looking up to see if it's raining, and a raindrop falls onto your forehead. I know that sounds a little crazy. If it hadn't happened to me, I would hardly believe it myself.

I sighed, relieved. Suddenly, I had no doubt at all: The universe, or the depths of my psyche, had chosen to answer me. The name Pajama Program was simple and perfect. I knew exactly what that meant and immediately got up out of my seat. It was the wrong stop for my meeting, but I didn't care. I left the subway and called Demo.

"I got it."

"You got what?" Demo asked.

"My purpose."

"Do you know what it means and what to do?" he asked gently. I was near tears. "I do!"

I felt confident, lighter, elated even. I knew something had changed.

Mind you, I hadn't figured out all the details yet—not by a long shot. I was still confused about what form the project would take. But there was a big difference: I saw it now. It was taking form, still morphing, yet real and already perfect. "Pajama Program." I felt I had to accept this name, and if I did, I would slowly begin to know what to do; everything would be revealed to me in time. It was a strange but comforting feeling.

I knew, deep in my bones, that my path had been laid out before me. All I had to do was follow it. Follow my instincts. I believed I was being led, and I trusted that inner voice. It was undeniable, crazy, and wonderful.

My excitement for my career was waning, and I felt a new swell in my heart for these children who needed pajamas and a book at bedtime, for the children who needed some kind of safe, comforting bedtime ritual, some form of a kiss and a hug and a tucking in.

I felt their need for love, and in doing so, I felt love myself. And there's no small amount of blessing in working to accomplish what we're here on earth to do. For all of *you* who have felt stuck, underwhelmed, and unfulfilled in your everyday lives, I have to tell you—your purpose is out there.

Actually, your purpose is inside you. I promise you it is. You just need to exercise a little faith and be open to it.

The Heart of the Matter

* Find *your* pajamas!

YOUR PURPOSE CAN show up anywhere, anytime, at any age. It can change your career, your work relationships, your personal life, or all of it! I used to think "finding your purpose" only happened to iconic game-changers like Leonardo da Vinci, Albert Einstein, Martin Luther King, Jr., the Dalai Lama, or Oprah! But when you are open to finding your purpose, you will recognize it.

Living with meaning changes everything for you, and for so many others who will be impacted by your actions. Believe in yourself; believe in miracles.

When you do find *your* pajamas, the important thing is to begin to take action. That's when you'll find the courage to believe in yourself and in the unlimited power your purpose gives you. Life takes unexpected turns, and if you are on your true path, you'll get through the rocky parts.

* Meditate, then look out for "raindrops."

INSPIRATION COMES IN many forms. It often shows up when you're sitting in silence. Sometimes it comes to us in dreams, or it can just as readily manifest itself when you're on the move, as it did for me. Inspiration usually delivers your "aha" moment—embrace it. We all hear voices or see signs that address the questions in our hearts and challenge what we think we know. What's missing—and how will I know when I find it?

Many of us feel there's something missing in our lives—and often, too, in our work. It's human nature to seek meaning, to feel we have a purpose on this earth. When I found my purpose, it changed everything—not only for the children who go to bed afraid and alone, but also for millions of people like me—people who connected to each other through their invisible connection to that little girl. We all want to share in doing something that extends beyond our own wants, something that soothes others and has a lasting impact.

* Get to the other side.

IT'S NOT ALWAYS easy to switch lanes, but it's the only way to move forward. You may feel conflicted, disloyal, and confused—I sure did! I've learned how scary a career and life change can be, but I always remembered that fateful question: "If this is my life for the next 30 years, is it enough?"

You don't need to see the whole path before you—you just need to take the first step and trust that the next ones will be revealed. You may doubt yourself at first and others may doubt you, but you'll also find people who will support you.

Chapter 5

"Please Don't Forget Me"

*M*y cell phone rang one early summer day in 2001. At that time, you couldn't see who was calling, but I always picked up since most often it would be someone asking if I could bring pajamas for their kids.

This time, it was the voice of a youngish-sounding person who identified herself as a reporter from *Parenting*, a national family magazine. "Are you the woman delivering pajamas to children in Harlem?" she asked.

"Uh, yes, that's me, I guess."

"May I interview you for a little story?"

Gulp. "Sure," I said.

Frankly, I was thrilled to fill her in and surprised she was interested in such a small endeavor. But the more people who knew about these children, the better.

For my raindrop-inspired "Pajama Program" idea to get to the next level, it needed a downpour of support. I had exhausted my circle of family and friends who already gave as much as they could. I needed the equivalent of a megaphone to reach more people.

The reporter told me it would be just a few lines, a rather short piece, and part of several items on a page. I had the feeling she was both amused and heartened to be writing about something "small." We kept talking, and she was mostly gathering facts, but when I told her the story about the little girl who didn't know what pajamas were, she warmed up instantly. It's amazing—whenever I tell that story, everyone seems to understand. They get it.

We spoke for a short amount of time—maybe 10 minutes. What was there to say, really, other than I was giving pajamas and books to children in need? She said she'd let me know when the article would run. This call was proof that no good idea can truly flourish in a vacuum. Like life itself, a good idea or a blessed intention needs to breathe. And the only way it can breathe is if it is given air—and a megaphone.

I was still making deliveries several times every week. I enjoyed seeing all the kids in general, but I had grown fond of a few places in particular. I began to understand the various circumstances under which these children were "in need" and why they didn't live with a mom or dad or other family members.

I also had formed bonds with the caring people who took care of these children. I was still learning things from them, such as that the word "orphanage" had been changed to "group home" so the kids wouldn't be teased and called "orphans." The thought broke my heart.

I also learned that most group homes have on-site schools because the kids aren't able to keep up with peers elsewhere who go home to parents, maybe even with a dog waiting to jump on them when they come home. Those reality checks were emotional for me to digest. These kids were denied lives they deserved, with daily fun and carefree activities they could share with all children, not just with other kids who were like them—alone, abandoned.

The separation of these children from others was so unfair, so unjust. It wasn't their fault. I'd look at their faces and swore I felt their pain at not having parents and a home of their own. I deeply empathized with what I believed they were feeling: "One day, someone will come back for me."

When the children received their pajamas, they always wanted to put them on right away, even if it was noon, because they were so warm and clean and fit well. When they got a book, sometimes they'd ask, "When do I have to give it back?" I would tell them it was theirs forever. And then I turned away so they wouldn't see me fight to hold back my tears.

The more I got to know the staff at each facility, the more stories I would hear. Heart-wrenching stories, like the one about five-year-old Joshua, who smuggled armfuls of our new, size three, girls' pajamas under his bed. Why? Because his mother repeatedly burned his little sister with her cigarettes until someone finally came and took the children out of her care. His sister was in the ICU, and he wanted to make sure she got enough warm pajamas.

The bright spirit of another child touched me immediately. This little girl, Isabella, recognized me at one of our reading events and remembered that I'd visited her group home with pajamas in the past. Her eyes lit up, and she asked me if I would visit again and bring her more pajamas. I thought to myself, "How is it possible that this little girl is without a mom or dad to tuck her into bed at night?"

She looked up at me and added, "When you bring pajamas, will you bring me some shoes, too?"

She tugged at my heart, and I promised her another visit with special pajamas, and for her, shoes!

"Please don't forget me," she added.

Forget her??? How could I? How could anyone?

I also read to a little boy named Roy every week. Some of the kids at group homes are fortunate enough to have a member of their family take them "home" for a weekend once in a while. On this particular Friday, another boy named Ronny was going home to his aunt's for a weekend visit, and he was thrilled.

Sitting beside me was Roy, who shared a cottage in the group home with Ronny. Roy and I were reading about bears when everyone heard Ronny's voice as he screamed, "I'm going home now!" and scooped up his stuff and headed into the waiting car.

Without saying a word, Roy leaned closer to me, put his arms around me, and gave me a big hug and a kiss on my cheek. My eyes began to tear up, and I held him for as long as I could. I guess at that moment for him, I was the closest thing to home.

———

THINGS WERE GETTING slowly but steadily better for my Pajama Program, and I was holding all my worlds together. Word of what I was doing for the children kept spreading among caregivers, and I was able to handle the growing "Needs Pajamas" list as more and more friends—and friends of friends—started sending me pajamas and books by the box-loads.

At this point, I was pretty much a robot at my day jobs. Sadly, I became one of those workers I despised—someone who did the least amount of work she could get away with. I couldn't believe that was me, a horrible person taking advantage of my bosses. I was filled with shame. But here I was, arms full of pajamas with barely any room to hold on to my job. *I can handle this.*

But I couldn't always handle what I saw at the shelters. It's agonizing enough to meet a group of children you know are dealing with abuse and abandonment, but to notice that some of them are black and blue from beatings, or have a broken arm from being yanked too hard, is painful beyond compare. I've often had to find a quiet corner away from everyone when I can't stop the tears. It's unimaginable what happens to some of these children, and although we read about it in the papers and see it on the news, when it's standing there in front of you, all of two feet tall, it's very real and very sickening.

I can't count the number of times I've thought about hiding a child under my coat and leaving. I've thought about stealing a baby who had blood on his clothes from a fight between his parents and taking home a teenage girl who didn't want to be transferred for the third time to a new group home in a different city.

All the deep breaths and trust in the system didn't help when I learned that that little boy stole pajamas for his sister in the ICU because their mother burned her with cigarettes.

———

I ALSO LEARNED mothers hurt, too. Sister Teresa "Tesa" Fitzgerald of the Sisters of Joseph in Queens taught me about babies with moms in prison. She also taught me how much I needed a mentor in a world where I, myself, was a baby. Every year, I am more and more inspired by her and her nonprofit organization, Hour Children. Staff members take the children to prisons to visit with their incarcerated moms for one hour every week—that's what the mothers and children are legally entitled to. Sister Tesa taught me that while the children deserved more than they were getting in life, these women also deserved a second chance so that they could regain control of their lives. And together, they deserved the chance to forge a mother–child bond. That bond was exactly what was missing for my Pajama Program kids at bedtime.

I was in awe of the amazing Sister Tesa. More than 25 years earlier, she'd asked a judge to allow her to take responsibility for bringing a baby to visit the mother in prison for one hour on a regular basis. The judge allowed it, and Hour Children, a program that keeps imprisoned mothers and their children connected, was born.

Talk about the power of one—she was, and is, a force. I am so grateful to Sister Tesa for being my first Pajama Program mentor. She taught me what the children we served had been through and what they needed now, and that provided me with not only an education but also a constant source of energy. Surely I could keep delivering pajamas if she was taking babies on buses to prisons every week.

As the program grew, I sought out another mentor, whose path was similar but was several steps ahead of me. Joi Gordon, CEO of Dress for Success, was someone I wanted in my life, and in my ear. Joi answered my call that first time and has done so every time since. She's happy to answer any question I have and brainstorm any idea I'm considering. Joi always motivated me because she was the perfect combination of heart and brains. She always spoke so passionately about the women her organization served, yet she knew she was running a business. Nonprofits are businesses, and many of us are so attached to our constituents that we forget that. Joi always answered my questions about staffing policies, insurance needs, and other practical matters while encouraging me to find new ways to support our kids and lead with my heart.

As she and her organization continue to skyrocket, she still makes room in her schedule for me, and I'm constantly inspired by her confidence, openness, and just plain smarts.

The Heart of the Matter

- Get close to the reasons you're doing what you're doing, and your heart will keep you focused.

IN MY CASE, the reasons had names: Joshua, Isabella, and Roy. Even when some of the children's tragic personal stories threatened to overwhelm me, I pressed forward. Keep your eye on the individual picture, and on the big picture, too. Your actions may feel small in the grand scheme of things you're working to change, but keep going.

- Mentors are key.

DON'T WAIT UNTIL you're falling off the ledge to ask for some advice. Forget pride, get over the embarrassment of asking for help, and beg for information—all you can get. When you connect with others engaged in similar issues, you'll learn valuable lessons—but more important, you'll be inspired. On those many days when you're thinking maybe you've set your sights too high, inspiration will propel you to new heights.

Chapter 6

When the World
Fell Apart

*N*othing can prepare you for the unthinkable. In the fall of
2001, I was gearing up for winter, or what I started calling
"Danger Season" because it's the coldest time of year for children.
And then . . . September 11.

That morning, I was at my desk in an office near the Empire
State Building doing some marketing work for a group of entre-
preneurs. We didn't have a TV or radio nearby, and back then it
wasn't commonplace for people (or at least me) to keep an eye on
news throughout the day. We started to hear a commotion outside
our door, and people were saying crazy things like "We have to
leave the building because planes might crash into the Empire
State Building next."

Our family and friends started calling to fill us in, but none of
us could imagine or grasp at first what anyone was talking about.

Within minutes, though, we were able to figure out what had happened, and we ran out with masses of people to the West Side Highway. From there, I walked—along with tens of thousands of people—to the opposite side of the bridge. Demo was there in his car, like so many others waiting for their loved ones marching north.

I remember my cell phone didn't ring as I walked. It was disturbingly silent; no one spoke. My thoughts were of getting through that day and then finding a way to live a life I really LOVED with people I truly cared about; that is, if we survived at all. It was a scary day for New Yorkers, and I couldn't look ahead any more than an hour at a time.

During the days that followed, I felt alone in my pajama mission. And it did feel extra tiny that September day. It took several weeks for me to let go of the 9/11 fear that paralyzed us and get down to the business of making changes in my life that would lead to a more purposeful existence where every day would count.

I mention 9/11 for a variety of reasons, but primarily because, even in the face of death and atrocity, when our faith in humanity was tested, I remained confirmed in my belief that there is enough. Enough love, laughter, joy, goodness . . . and in that terrible time, I realized my mission was all the more significant. Bad things happen. But with determination and doggedness, so can the good. Life after that day made me realize that it truly is the "little things" that change lives. I would help those in need in my little way, because the world was full of need. Whatever doubts I may have had about Pajama Program were entirely put to rest.

As things began to return to a new kind of normal, Demo and I continued our collecting, buying, and boxing up of pajamas and books, delivering them all over New York City and Westchester. A few months into this strange new year, *Parenting* magazine followed up to say my article, which had been delayed nearly a year, would finally run in their December 2002/January 2003 double issue.

"OK," I said. "That's great."

The issue came out with a tiny article in it. It was on a top right corner in the "Giving Back" section with a photo of knitted baby booties. And it was really an "item," as the reporter had implied, not an article. It said all kids deserved a pair of pajamas while listening to a bedtime story, and it gave our phone number for more information.

I never thought it would get noticed in a big way. Really, it was nice, but it was just about 60 words.

And yet, as for what happened within days, "nice" doesn't cover it! How about overwhelming, unbelievable, astonishing, miraculous, and phenomenal?

For months after September 11, it seemed that generosity and compassion permeated everything. Was there anything more important than being generous and taking care of one another in the months after the attack? There was nothing we wouldn't do for each other—especially for the children, as it turned out.

As soon as that magazine hit newsstands, the entire country was sending me boxes and packages, bundles and sacks, priority Jiffy bags and FedEx letters. The moment I set foot in my apartment's lobby, I was bombarded by the building staff: "You have too many packages filling up our closets. You have to take them upstairs right now." "What are these boxes, anyway?" "Please take all these sacks of letters, everything now. We must clear it all out."

I had no idea what they were talking about. The doorman and some other men he apparently recruited were shoving packages at me and piling up boxes at my feet in front of the elevator. I was totally confused and had started pulling the boxes into the elevator with me. My head was spinning. They had no idea what was in the packages and neither did I. It's a wonder the elevator didn't crash due to the weight.

I had to get everything out of the elevator and into my apartment on the third floor. I went up and down many, many times before I stopped to rest and open one of the packages. It felt soft and was in a beige padded envelope. There was a pair of pajamas in it and a handwritten note asking me to give them to a child. I still couldn't figure out who the sender was, but as I started to unwrap and open more and more mailings, someone's note or letter mentioned the *Parenting* magazine article and the light bulb went on.

On one of my trips back down to the lobby, Demo came in and was startled when he saw me frantically loading the elevator. He ran to help me. "You'll see," I told him. When we got upstairs, he took a look at the pile and tentatively peered into a few of the boxes I had opened. He was baffled.

"*Parenting* magazine came out," I said. And he smiled.

That evening, I never would've imagined that it was only the first day's "take," and that there was much more to come. We kept opening and reading and crying.

In the weeks that followed, the packages kept pouring in. When I tell you thousands of deliveries came to my co-op in Riverdale every day, I am probably underestimating the number. The doorman was having a fit, and the other apartment owners were outraged that there was no room for their packages in the storage rooms. They all wanted to know what the heck was going on. I thought I was going to get kicked out of the building.

I didn't tell any of my neighbors what I was doing with all these packages. I was afraid of what they might say. And I was embarrassed. Did they think I was stupid enough to think that pajamas were going to solve the very real problems of these children? Would they think my idea was naïve, even idiotic? Would I catch them laughing behind my back?

As I remained secretive about what I was doing, an ugly thought poked at me: *Was* I just a ridiculous person with a "cute" idea? No, that wasn't it. My reasons for not sharing this work, and what was in those boxes, was partly to protect nameless children—but it was also part self-preservation. The idea that these beautiful children were going to sleep—or *trying* to go to sleep—in their soiled and too-tight clothes was killing me inside. Just thinking about what they had been through was torture for me. I knew the pajamas were comforting them, and I didn't want anyone to tell me otherwise.

My project may not have been saving the world, but it lived in my heart along with these kids, and I desperately needed to protect it from strangers. I didn't trust that my neighbors would be as sympathetic as the readers of the magazine who "got it." I thought they might think I was just plain crazy. And honestly, I wasn't sure that I wasn't. I was a ball of emotions every day, feeling alone and vulnerable, crying at the drop of a hat. This was my first real experience with strangers who wanted to help. I steered clear of everyone in the building because I knew I couldn't tell them that it would soon be under control, or that it was an organized program, or that I had a plan that didn't involve their having to weave their way through the mounds of my unwieldy packages in the mailroom. Most of all, I couldn't tell them how exciting it was to be getting so many pajamas!

From that first night of deliveries onward, we were trapped in a sea of cardboard boxes. Demo and I couldn't even see each other through a thicket of brown packaging in our apartment.

Box after box was filled with new pajamas—books, too—and some letters held cash.

I remember one note very clearly. The handwritten note came with a single dollar bill: *"I want to help you to buy another pajama."* That note hit me hard. Holding that envelope, I felt I was in the room with the person who wrote the message. I imagined the note, written in shaky handwriting, came from a senior citizen who'd taken a dollar from her meager food budget in order to help the children I was serving. Maybe she, too, had spent time in a shelter or orphanage. This was personal to her. And she trusted me.

Demo and I cried together for days as we opened the mail—our hearts filled to almost bursting—and we both had the same thought: "People are counting on us."

Until then, only a few people knew about Pajama Program, and I knew most of those people. I was able to keep a grasp on the program, even as my paper files and to-do list grew and grew. But when I started getting deliveries from strangers, I realized Pajama Program wasn't just "mine" anymore. It belonged to every single person who sent me something in those letters, padded envelopes, and boxes. I was now responsible to every one of them to GET THIS JOB DONE! They were counting on me because I had made an announcement to the world that I was doing this "thing." Strangers trusted me without even knowing me. That was scary. No questions asked. They gave freely, and generously.

Letter after letter reinforced my belief that there was indeed a need, and also that there would be help and support for me to do something about it. My intention had become steel-clad; I felt it in my gut. Strangers knew I was on to something—they felt it, too.

The human connection was tangible.

Slow was not the pace at which I could proceed any longer. I felt a rush—both emotionally but also in how I moved from that day forward. Everything had to be done at Mach speed—especially opening and organizing all that was being delivered. This trust from supporters is as sacrosanct today as it was when I read those first letters.

I was living in what felt like a storage room and still feeling like a neophyte in terms of creating any kind of organization. But I believed strongly that I was on the right track and that I would naturally know how to move from one day to the next, how to make the right decisions, where to go for help, and how not to break down before I was done.

Weeks went by with boxes of pajamas and books showing up every day, and I began to think more about choices. Every day, I knew I had a choice. I could keep going, turn back, or change course. The decision was mine. I could come home and collapse (if I could find a cleared space to curl up in), or Demo and I could keep hauling boxes upstairs, hoping our neighbors wouldn't throw a fit.

———

EVERY NIGHT, DEMO and I hoisted boxes up on top of the highest ones already stacked. We marked the new ones with the date in a different color marker. Most evenings boxes and packages were piled up to the ceiling.

I knew from past experience with my neighbors that the boxes in the hallway might perturb some of them. When I had holiday parties in my apartment, guests would spill into the hall, chatting, drinks in hand. I always tried to offer drinks and snacks to the neighbors to make up for it, but some of them didn't want to participate and I was asked to confine my guests to my apartment. I guess I would've felt the same way, and I did my best to corral my friends, but sometimes it didn't work.

There was a good chance I would get pushback on this, too,

but I had no choice. I had to take that chance. I was quickly placing the boxes up and down the hallways, worrying about my neighbors' reactions any minute. But I also thought, "How could anyone have a problem?" They were for children—children who, unlike my neighbors, were cold at night and didn't have warm pajamas to sleep in.

We worked very hard to keep the pile-up and sorting process contained to three or four hours every evening so few people would be inconvenienced, but we did have a couple grunt and grumble as they walked around the stacks. Nobody asked us for an explanation, so I didn't explain, and I didn't make eye contact, but I did say "sorry, sorry, sorry, sorry, sorry" all night long.

Back inside the apartment, Demo and I created pathways between the boxes so we could get around. We'd lose sight of each other, calling out: "Are you here somewhere? Which room are you in? I brought pizza." "Where do you want to eat? On the short boxes in the living room or should we throw a tablecloth over the stacks of FedExes on the sofa?" We found ourselves engulfed in our own little storage unit, built on the generosity of others and our own determination.

My brother Laurence reminded me that a local morning drive radio DJ, "Goumba Johnny" on WPLJ, went to our high school the same time I did and suggested that maybe he would help me. His show was full of fun and pranks and attracted a big audience who wanted to wake up every morning to unpredictable mayhem and amusement.

I didn't know this DJ, as his much cooler high school existence never intersected with my nerd trajectory, but I was open to contacting anyone who might lend a hand. I immediately wrote to the DJ explaining our connection and my plight. I needed volunteers to help with all our sorting and delivering. He called me! He said he wanted to help and would be happy to interview me on the air about what I was doing. I was beyond excited and tried to remain calm as he asked questions and I answered LIVE on the air. This was a major New York area station, so it was a big deal to me.

Later that morning, I received a call from a young woman named Ana who was a devout listener of the station and fan of the DJ.

"I heard you on the morning show, and I want to help you," she said. There was something in the purity and sureness of her voice that linked my soul to hers, and I was anxious to meet her.

Our in-person connection was instantaneous. I was impressed by her confidence, but what I loved even more was that she wore her heart on her sleeve. Ana took on the new role of "New York Chapter President." She had a full-time job with a demanding schedule but volunteered to help with whatever administrative and computer tasks I had.

"Don't worry, I'll take care of it all on the weekends," she told me. And that was the beginning of a relationship that continues—16 years later—today. Ana showed me that there were indeed other busy New Yorkers who were passionate about children having pajamas and could help me make this thing real, concrete, and permanent.

Ana wasn't the only Pajama Program angel I heard from in 2004. A woman named Geri called me, too, after hearing me on the radio. At the time, there was only Pajama Program New York, and she said, "I'm in New Jersey. Can I open a New Jersey chapter for you?"

"Sure," I said. "That would be great!"

"What should I do?" she asked.

"I have no idea," I answered.

I was unaware of what Geri's life had been like, what her struggles were, and why she felt compelled to call me right then. But there was something in Geri's voice that was vulnerable that day, and I felt like I wanted to help her as much as she wanted to help me. We met face-to-face, and I was right: We had connected for a powerful reason.

Over the next few months, she shared some of her personal story with me. She and her devoted husband of 50-plus years raised a wonderful son, Paul. Their lives were full of adventure and fun as the three of them journeyed through life together. But, she told me, her health had deteriorated, and physical complications had stifled her mobility. She never wanted to give up her zest for living and was determined to fight her way back to enjoying life. It became harder and harder for her to remain positive until one day when she said a prayer and vowed to find something to give her meaning and a reason to keep fighting. That's when she turned on the radio and heard me talking about Pajama Program.

Geri figured out how to start a New Jersey chapter and she ran it like a pro, organizing PJ drives and delivering them all over the state. Geri was also an ace at getting the press to pay attention to her Pajama Program chapter, and within months she received a call from a mysterious woman who happened to manufacture pajamas and knew of an empty space ripe for a NJ home base. The chapter soon had its very own Pajama Program Reading Center in Red Bank on the grounds of Poricy Park, where it remains today.

Ana and Geri were now helping me start a new family. Soon we would welcome another helping hand, someone who magically appeared from my past.

In 1998, when I first started out, I was buying maybe 20 pairs of pajamas a week and dropping them off at one shelter. By 2002, I was buying 100 or more per week, including adult sizes for the teens, and spending nearly $1,000, easily—and that didn't include postage for shipping. I covered about 40 shelters and group homes (orphanages) within a 60-mile radius of New York City.

After the *Parenting* magazine article appeared in 2003, boxes full of pajamas started arriving, so I could rein in my personal spending, finally. I was thrilled—yet terrified. How would I get all these PJs to the shelters? Before, my fear had been that I'd run out of pajamas before I ran out of children. Ana and Geri hit the ground running in 2004 with PJ drives, and I was suddenly worried about the opposite: Would I always find enough kids to wear all of these pajamas? And would I do it fast enough, before our apartment was so full there was nowhere to live?

Unbeknownst to me, our local Riverdale newspaper received a call about my deliveries of pajamas and books to children in need. A reporter phoned me to confirm this and said they wanted to publish a story to help me spread the word. When the article appeared, I received several packages of pajamas and also a small notecard in the mail, which read:

Hello Genevieve,

I don't know if you remember me or not, but we both went to Fordham and worked at WFUV radio there. I, too, live in Riverdale. I read about your project and I have just started my own PR firm. If you are interested, I would like to represent you pro bono so I can get some experience and client work under my belt.

Here is my number—

Sincerely,
Jennefer

Ah, I thought. There really *is* enough!

I read Demo the note. He said, "Last week you told me you needed PR! And do you know what you did last week when you told me that? You raised your fist, shook it at the world, and made a bold declaration. And you got what you needed! That is your body language expressing your determination! You need to raise your fist with the same force every time you need something, and it'll come to you. The universe will support you, if you are on purpose. In your life, both the visible and invisible forces show up to support your true work."

He dashed to his computer right then and there and printed out this quotation, which has been attributed by some people to William Hutchison Murray, a Scottish mountaineer. I framed it, and it's on my desk to this day:

> Until one is committed, there is hesitancy, the chance to draw back . . . Concerning all acts of initiative (and creation), there is one elementary truth the ignorance of which kills countless ideas and splendid plans: that the moment one definitely commits oneself, then Providence moves too. All sorts of things occur to help one that would never otherwise have occurred. A whole stream of events issues from the decision, raising in one's favor all manner of unforeseen incidents and meetings and material assistance, which no man could have dreamed would have come his way. Whatever you can do, or dream you can do, begin it. Boldness has genius, power, and magic in it. Begin it now.

And I did. Quickly, I called Jennefer. "Yes, I remember you," I nearly shouted, "and yes, I'd love your help!"

Soon, Jennefer and I met. She was as pretty as she'd been almost 20 years before. Since graduation, she'd worked for a large PR firm in New York City but had recently decided to start her own company. Pajama Program was her first client! She seemed extremely efficient, smart as a whip, buttoned up, and a bit compulsive—in the best way possible.

Jennefer quickly crafted concise descriptions of our work, wrote up stories about the children we served, and put together our "A" list of local and national press contacts. How did she know exactly what we wanted to tell the world? The first thing she did was join me to meet some of the groups who received pajamas and books! It didn't take Jen long to say what I was feeling in my heart: "I want to take these kids home."

Jennefer got right to work trying every way she could to secure a Pajama Program mention in a little magazine called O. I thought she was pretty ambitious—it was Oprah's publication, after all—but she kept at it, committed and convinced. She believed!

It was victory for Jennefer! I remember the day she told me I had an interview with a reporter from O at their headquarters. She was beyond excited and, of course, so was I. As I headed to the magazine's office, I was petrified that I'd tell them my story and they'd be indifferent. I was convinced they heard "nice" stories all the time and wouldn't find this one to be special at all. But when the writer asked me her final Oprah-esque question, "So what was your aha moment?," I gulped. This interviewer was interested indeed, and I knew it right then—my little story was going to get into O magazine. In April 2005, the article about Pajama

Program appeared in O magazine and soon we had 20 more chapters throughout the country and, you guessed it, lots more boxes!

———

"I NEED A space just for these pajamas. I have to get organized!" I exclaimed to Demo, raising my fist purposefully and boldly, once again.

On my trips delivering pajamas, I'd often stick around to read to the children. It was exhilarating but exhausting. I'd beg Demo to pick me up at our local train station and then give me the car for a few hours. Or, even better, I'd cajole him into playing chauffeur for the night. I would jam as much as I could into our Camry and drive around all evening, making my drop-offs.

All the caregivers I met at my stops were thrilled and helpful, and they would carry the boxes and bags from my car, through the parking lots, and into the rooms and cottages for the children. Pajamas were always needed for children who weren't there on my last visit. Sadly, children were often coming and going, as they were transferred to another facility, out of state, maybe closer to relatives, or perhaps to a foster family for a trial run in hopes of it being a good fit. I hate writing these words, "trial run" and "good fit." It makes my stomach turn. Too often my pajamas went to children who were being processed into the foster care system for the first time. To this day, thinking about children being "processed" pierces my heart. Meat is processed, not children.

One day, I arrived at ANDRUS's children's home in Yonkers with an especially packed car. My contact there, Shirley, came out with a big smile and took a look inside the Camry. Her eyes widened.

"Wow, big delivery today! That's fantastic. Thank you so much."

I looked in and saw, as if for the first time, how much I'd actually squeezed into my car. I was amazed, and all of a sudden very weary. I guess I sighed, loudly, and Shirley paused, watching me. It was clear she had something to say.

"Genevieve, wouldn't you like a home base for yourself? A place where people deliver donations, maybe a place to have the kids come and get their pajamas and books, where they could sit and read with you?"

"I would love it," I said, "but where would I get the money to rent a place like that?"

The thought of a "stationary place" had never even occurred to me but I was learning that sometimes divine intervention had its own way of creeping in. I guess I was just moving all the time, trying to fit everything in, and my brain just didn't have the time or bandwidth to find a better way on its own. I was winging it, all day, every day. I've learned sometimes that's exactly when a solution finds you.

"You know, we actually have an enclosed porch here," Shirley said, gesturing toward the door of the cottage that was home for the youngest boys. "It's very rundown and dirty, a mess really, but I think we could give it to you if you want to fix it up."

"Give it to me?! A home base?" I don't remember if I actually said those words out loud!

I couldn't believe what I was hearing. This untethered, wild idea of mine could actually find footing at a former orphanage and have an address?

Oh yes, it could! My contractor brother Frank took us on as his priority and made it happen. He led the next several months of work by family, friends, and newfound volunteers and turned a little abandoned porch into a beautiful Reading Center filled with shelves of new books, colorful tables and chairs to sit and read, walls painted with fantasy storybook characters, and bins and bins of new pajamas in all sizes and colors. My pajamas and I finally had a home.

No matter your age, once you stepped into our Pajama Program Reading Center where stories came alive and magic was possible, you were a child again. Our beautiful room filled with love every afternoon when children from group homes came to read with us—and get their new pajamas, of course.

On Wednesdays, seven-year-old Jared's group read with us. One particular day, I noticed Jared had two books with him as he walked in. He plopped down beside me, asked, "Do you know who this is?," and then shouted, "BAM, BAM, BAM! Kick it up a notch!"

He was so adorable, imitating Emeril Lagasse's signature phrase! Jared's round face and chubby cheeks were morphing into Emeril's right in front of me.

"It's that chef on TV, right?!" I answered with a big grin.

"It's Emeril, and I want to be a chef like him!"

This boy had found his purpose! He pushed the two big books into my lap. They were Emeril's cookbooks, of course. "I can read those," he said, looking me straight in the eyes. I had no doubt.

Several weeks later, Demo called me from the set he was working at. "Fun day today. We're doing a commercial with Chef Emeril."

"WHAT?" I nearly jumped out of my skin. I relayed my Jared story.

He came home that night with a surprise, an autographed cookbook: "To Jared, my friend and chef of the future!! BAM, BAM! Love, Emeril."

Demo said he's never had a hug as hard as the day he handed that gift to Jared.

Sammy, another boy, was about six and read with us every Friday afternoon. One day, I peered out of our door onto the vast court-yard and saw him racing toward me wild with excitement, waving something black in his hand.

"Miss Genny, Miss Genny, I need a lot of pajamas today, a real lot!" He ran hard into my arms, elated and out of breath. "Here's a garbage bag to put them in!"

I didn't know what was causing this excitement, but I wanted him to know I was thrilled, too. "Oh boy! What's happening, Sammy?"

"I have a foster family! And they're coming to pick me up today!"

Together we stuffed the big black bag with pajamas. "These, and these, and these, too, PLEEEASE."

He paused and looked at me. In his eyes I saw a little boy who wished for so long to feel special and wanted. I knew I'd prob-ably never see him again because today his wish was coming true. To Sammy, a foster family was a promise of a mom and dad, a real home, a real school, friends and baseball, loving, laughing, and get-ting tucked in at bedtime. This was his dream, the dream of so many boys and girls in group homes. Yes, absolutely yes, he could have all the pajamas he wanted.

Watching Sammy drag that heavy bag across the lawn to wait for his foster family, I let the tears flow. I knew he wanted those pajamas so he'd be ready for all the bedtime hugs he was going to get now. He was hauling precious cargo. He had his pajamas, and with each pair he had hope.

The Heart of the Matter

- You'll never be prepared for the unexpected.

YOU MAY FEEL vulnerable, and that is OK. There are times when it's up to you, alone, to make it happen. And then there are times you have to know that you're not in it alone. There are seen and unseen forces by your side, and you have to hold on for dear life and trust.

- Share your story.

SHARING HOW A pivotal aha moment has led you to a new life and a new cause can attract angels, an onslaught of surprise, and welcome deliveries, a new home base, or more. That blurb in *Parenting* magazine changed a lot for us—and for the neighbors in our apartment building! But when I started getting deliveries from strangers, I realized Pajama Program wasn't just "mine" anymore, it belonged to Ana, Geri, Jennefer, Shirley, and every single person who sent letters, pajamas, and money to support our cause.

- Make the commitment.

YOUR UNWAVERING DEVOTION to your goal combined with a deep desire to find a way to make it happen have the extraordinary power to bring your dream to fruition. Believe me, I know this takes practice and . . . commitment!

Chapter 7

Dangerous Sacrifices

*B*elieving is hard work to keep up 24/7 and having faith is not always easy, but the trick is not to let fear undermine your belief. The completion of our Reading Center at ANDRUS in Yonkers was thrilling, and I felt like my Pajama Program was gaining some momentum. But still, I personally needed to have a clear sign that this work so many were now "feeling" along with me meant something deep—that we were really and truly filling a significant need. I wanted to know we were changing the lives of these children, even in a small way.

I have learned a million times that when I have a conviction that what I am doing is the right thing for children, and what I am asking for will help us achieve our goal, the answers come to my door or to my phone.

On the day of our Reading Center grand opening in July 2004, an announcement ad donated by a generous marketing agency appeared in the local newspaper. I received a call from a man who said he saw the ad and wanted to learn more. He asked a lot of questions fast. "What is Pajama Program? Who are you giving the pajamas and books to? Why are you giving pajamas?" I was taken aback but did my best to answer without even taking a breath to ask for his name or why he was calling even though I felt unsettled. I had no idea what he wanted, and I tried not to be defensive, but it felt like I was being interrogated.

Finally, he became quiet and said, "I'm asking so many questions because I lived at the ANDRUS orphanage when I was a little boy. I know how hard the nights are when you have no mom or dad."

My defenses collapsed, and my heart started racing. I had a million questions.

His name was Dave. At six years old, he was taken by his grandparents to the orphanage where his older brother already was living. They could no longer care for him, and his parents had decided to pursue their own separate lives. "I was scared and confused," he told me.

What could it have felt like to be "dropped off" with no word about why, or when he could go home or who would come and visit him? Who would do that to a child, or two children?

Now, at age 46, Dave told me he owned a successful bus company and a martial arts school. He married, raised a family of his own, and worked very hard to reunite with his parents. He was determined to find answers to try and heal emotions that still ran deep.

He wanted to learn about Pajama Program and decided it was finally time to revisit ANDRUS to come to terms with his past. I felt that my core belief, that our Pajama Program concept could actually help these children, was going to be put to the test. I knew he had the answer.

Dave visited us at the Pajama Program Reading Center one Saturday, and together we toured the ANDRUS grounds. The fruit trees that were only fragile young sprouts when Dave lived on campus are fully grown today. The brown and green field beyond was in Dave's time and is still a playground for the children, as well as turkeys and deer. Adjacent to the field is the small brick elementary school where children walked to from their cottages, which were arranged in a semicircle around another big lawn. The main house serves as the entrance of the campus, welcoming incoming children and visitors, the same as it did all those years ago when Dave first arrived. I could tell the tour of the grounds caused his memories to flood back. I could actually feel the tumultuous emotions running through his body as we walked together in silence.

I didn't know anything about this man, and I didn't know how to comfort him. He stood six feet tall and appeared strong, but I could feel him as a little boy next to me. I waited for him to speak. I desperately wanted to know what memories he was reliving, why he thought today was the day for him to return here, and why I was the one to witness it. As we walked around the outside of the children's cottages, he chuckled and told me how he and the other boys would sneak down to what was then the piggery to feed the pigs. He told me they also snuck around their cottages after midnight sometimes when the house mother went to sleep! He suddenly stopped and stared. We had found his cottage.

He took a long minute to look at it before he headed for the door. "Let's go in," he whispered. I didn't know what to expect, what he would find there, or what he would feel. I knew what I was feeling, and it was pure anxiety. We climbed the stairs slowly to where his bedroom was. I could only imagine what he was thinking as he peered in. He bravely entered the room and said softly, "I cried myself to sleep, missing my mother."

And right then I got the answer I had been searching for. Dave was revisiting childhood wounds and painful memories, and that was the only way I could actually see and feel how Pajama Program really helped these children. He said the pajamas and books we were giving to the children meant more than I would ever know, that nighttime was such a lonesome time for a child living among strangers and that cozy pajamas made them feel good and warm and special. He remembered bedtime and the pain. He told me we were making a difference. I knew it in my core, but I always yearned for proof. Now I had it.

He said there were times he didn't think he would ever go home again, and he said camaraderie with the other boys grew in time. "We became brothers," he told me. He began to feel safe at ANDRUS. He felt like he belonged somewhere.

A few months after we met and Dave reconnected with ANDRUS, he was asked to give the commencement speech there. Although he'd come through so many fires, this was a different challenge. What he wanted to say would be emotional. Dave didn't relish the thought of possibly losing control and fighting back tears. A few sentences into his speech, we watched a man talk about the boy who was left there on those grounds, the boy who was taken out of his home and placed into a foreign environment with strangers caring for him. Right then at that podium he came to grips with his past and really came home—to himself, and to the life he had built from the scraps he'd rescued.

This hit home for me. Was I also trying to rescue myself? Did I need these children to fill my heart, take the place of children I never had? Did I have to learn there's support for every one of us from each other, and also from the universe? I was keyed into one big truth: None of us is alone. We have the most sacred of all connections right in front of us—the human connection. And together we are all welcome to many invisible connections from the universe.

As I listened to Dave speak, I felt a kinship with him. Somehow I understood, on a deep level, how it felt for him to feel alone, abandoned. I had a family who loved me, I knew, but I also had a hole in my life, one I was so desperate to fill. In a way, perhaps selfishly, I let Dave help fill it.

——

PAJAMA PROGRAM WAS really gaining momentum. Something had been triggered inside me, something deep and primal, and it was propelling us forward at a feverish pace. What was it that had drawn me to those children initially and now had a life of its own?

On paper, I'd been convinced that my life was everything I'd ever wanted. But life isn't lived on paper. It's lived through action, as directed by our hearts and minds. As time went on and the years passed, I realized in spite of myself that I was working to make other people richer and happier. I wasn't really helping anyone who needed it. This hard truth began to trouble me in quietly insistent ways.

A deeply spiritual connection was forming between me and those whom I could help, and not solely because I benefited from the act of giving. I was benefiting from having found, and then beginning to fulfill, my life's mission. And there's no small amount of blessing in working to accomplish what we're here on earth to do.

I'd finally chosen to focus on only one project at my day job, and

I chose an importing company in Manhattan. I worked about 40 hours a week, but I was able to make my own schedule and include weekends so I could dedicate some weekdays to Pajama Program. At work, I kept my cell phone hidden on my waist so I wouldn't miss someone trying to contact me asking for pajamas or where to drop off donations. When I felt my phone buzz, I had to find a quiet corner to take the call and whisper so clients wouldn't hear me. All these calls for me were urgent, and they were all I could think about. My job? What job?

The UPS guy and I were buddies. I'm sure he thought I was doing a bang-up job for my boss. I stowed away empty boxes in the back rooms where no one could see them and used them to pack my pajamas and send them off on the sly—making sure my boss wasn't around to catch me.

After that one mess with the sloppily packed box of materials, I was super careful to pay more attention to my work. Thankfully, I was usually on the floor alone, the others downstairs in the office. And miraculously I was still drawing a steady paycheck, the one thing that kept me tied to the corporate world, at least for the time being.

Still, every day at work I answered calls for pajamas on my cell phone, and accumulated PJs and books any way I could. I was spending my own salary on most of these items, plus shipping to several states outside New York and New Jersey, and I was constantly asking friends and family members to volunteer or buy more pajamas and books for the children. Some made the purchases, and some gave me cash. They told their friends and spread the word. I spoke to everyone I met about these children. But I was running ragged and my brain was all over the place at my day job. My boss kept asking me why I wasn't finishing my work.

———

BY NOW, I was getting into serious debt—$1,000 or more every couple of weeks showed up loud and clear on my credit card statement, and I was getting nervous. So was Demo. I was still delivering pajamas three or four nights every week, roughly 25 pairs per stop, all over Westchester County and up and down the island of Manhattan. Even with volunteers, I was handling most of the deliveries. By then, I'd say we were well over 5,000 pajamas distributed, and yet I still wasn't hitting most of my list. I didn't keep records early on, since I was using all my own money. When I started receiving financial donations from *Parenting* magazine readers, I did start keeping track, though the formal recordkeeping didn't start until we filed for our 501(c)(3).

I was running as fast as I could, but my handwritten "Needs Pajamas" list was growing, and it plagued me day and night. Calls were coming from people around the country with the same question: "Can I help in my city?" "Yes! Yes!" I responded. But without a clear outline of what I wanted chapter presidents to do, I trusted each person to come back to me with their own plan for their own city. To this day, I know that was one of the best decisions I ever made. Although I made it on the fly, I trusted my instinct that I was attracting honest and loving individuals to this work. Within weeks, we were up to 34 volunteer chapter presidents!

But now my day job was tottering on the line, and I truly thought I might be fired. I had been a model employee for most of my career—it's how I was raised and how I acted in all my prior jobs—so it was very uncomfortable for me. I felt conflicted.

I realized all my jobs had been a waste of time in the real scheme of things, and I was annoyed that I still had to keep clocking in. But

I needed the money. Hundreds, maybe thousands of children were in my pajamas at night, but it still wasn't enough.

I prayed the children were sleeping well, because I certainly wasn't.

Needless to say, this whole period was a very intense time. I was going, going, going all the time—days, nights, weekends, you name it. Demo tried to get me to rest, but I never listened. Even if I stopped physically, my brain was going a mile a minute. It was hard for anyone—even Demo—to get my attention unless they were talking about Pajama Program. I wasn't the best company in those days.

Even my husband—that paragon of spiritual generosity and warmth—was beginning to lose his patience. I expected him to be at my continual beck and call. He was happy to help with deliveries and the like, but we needed more and more pajamas and books. There was shopping and packing to do all the time, and I constantly turned to Demo to help. Boxes needed to be unpacked, counted, sorted, and recorded, then boxed up in new boxes (boxes are expensive) and shipped. Our shipping bills were sky high. "Charge cards!" I thought. "There's always plastic!"

I lied to Demo each time I said I'd make a credit card bill payment with my next paycheck. Now I was spending all my money on pajamas, my bills going deeper into arrears. I offered my husband no option for discussion about my choices. As an actor, Demo's take-home pay was unpredictable; we'd always counted on two salaries. I didn't care that I was being irresponsible, and I didn't care if it was wrong. This was definitely my low point as a partner.

As I became busier, we fought about how I was obsessed and couldn't be calm or understand that these things take time and there's no rush. Demo said I was "pushing" all the time, not allowing the universe to do its part to meet me halfway. But I wasn't listening to him, and it was very frustrating for him to continue to be there for me 24/7. Of course, I was unhappy with his attitude.

I was preoccupied, and sometimes downright intolerable when it came to doing what I wanted to do. When I needed a desk for my Pajama work, I bought a computer and desk and put it right smack in the middle of our bedroom without consulting Demo. I did this despite the fact that I'd only begrudgingly conceded to his putting his desk in the living room of our apartment when we first started living together. I'd told him I never wanted a desk in my living room or bedroom, that these were sacred rooms that should not be invaded by work. How quickly I dismissed my own rule.

Many days and nights I was holed up in our bedroom on the computer feeling like a heel but at the same time forging ahead to get through the emails and letters to keep Pajama Program going.

I felt bad sitting at my "command center" in our bedroom, while Demo squeezed into a chair surrounded by stacks of pajama boxes in the living room. But it was otherwise easy for me to block out everything and everyone when I was in my "on a mission" mode. I saw my vision, even if Demo didn't. I was selfish and I took advantage of his support, I know. But he could fend for himself; these children could not. I wasn't wavering. Nothing and no one was going to stop me and my Pajama Program. It wasn't just a dream anymore; it was as real as the faces of each and every child I met and those I'd never meet. My marriage could be fixed later, I told myself. First things first.

Sometimes tunnel vision is a good thing, but not always, especially not when someone you love is standing beside you talking to you and you don't hear a word.

Pajama Program was taking over my life, and I was worried that any warm and fuzzy feelings my husband felt for me would disappear. It was hard for Demo while I was in my "me, me, me, pajama, pajama, pajama" phase. All he wanted was what any husband deserves: a wife who is present in the marriage. All I heard were restrictions he was putting on me and reasons why we couldn't do this or that. He said I was taking advantage of him. I denied it every time, but of course, he was right. I not only expected him to pay all the bills, I also asked him to pick up boxes, deliver boxes, chauffeur me to shelters, accompany me to every event, and meet every single person who organized a pajama drive. Oh, and smile through every minute.

Demo said I was losing touch with the reality of our life and the responsibilities of my partnership with him. When he confronted me about my financial responsibility to the marriage, I knew he had a point, but I argued back that his early support of me "finding my purpose" is what got us here in the first place. I insisted I'd find a way. I told him, "I can always work at McDonald's at night," and I repeated that many, many times until I convinced myself I might have to soon.

We'd vowed from the start to make our marriage full of unique experiences we'd share together. We had plans to enjoy our careers, travel the world, and entertain in a beautiful home we designed together. Now here we were sweating everything—especially the small stuff.

Month to month, we weren't sure how we'd survive, but for me there was no alternative: I had to live my life's purpose. I'd found the thing that gave me meaning and fulfillment. I had to give a hundred percent to Pajama Program and the kids.

The Heart of the Matter

- Leave juggling to the clowns.

WARNING: JUGGLING YOUR marriage or partnership, your finances, or your responsibilities will cause tension for you and probably others. Even when you have the best intentions, fooling yourself into thinking you won't drop any balls can result in jeopardizing something sacred. Proceed with caution.

- Recognize the boomerang effect.

HELPING OTHERS HAS a profound effect most of us don't expect. When you find your purpose, a deeply spiritual connection forms between you and those you are serving. You are focused on giving, yet you will realize that you are healing as a result. When Dave took me on the heartbreaking tour of his former orphanage, I felt the emotions emanating from him. But soon I knew that through his tears, I was also feeling the answer to my burning question about the value of my purpose.

Chapter 8

The Real
Meaning of Life

With all the time I was spending on Pajama Program, my job was getting increasingly challenging to manage, especially as the company went through a difficult time. My guilt-induced diligence saved my job, but I didn't know how long I could last. Then I came up with an idea that might satisfy both my boss and me. I suggested moving to part-time for a few months, which could save them some money and help them get back on track.

My boss liked the idea. Next, the hard part: I had to talk to Demo. He didn't like the idea. "Well, how are we going to keep covering all your credit card bills for the pajamas and books when we can hardly cover the rent as it is?" he wanted to know. But after much cajoling (begging), he relented. I swore on our marriage that I would find a way to bring in money for some of our bills (I reminded him of my McDonald's promise).

I had no idea how I could make part-time work financially, and I also didn't know how the company would eventually do or what would be next for me if I took this chance. I was really scared, but I couldn't dwell on the fears. If I could curb some of my personal Pajama Program expenses by filing as an official nonprofit, maybe I could attract some grant money. I could stop racking up personal debt, which had reached about $20,000 (and counting) on high-interest credit cards—and I could keep my promise to Demo to pitch in. I also vowed to myself to relax a bit and be more appreciative of everything he was doing for me.

So much had changed since that day a few years previously when I brought pajamas to the shelter and met that little girl. The world had changed. *I* had changed. My marriage had changed. I had half a job, barely, but Demo's work was flooding in, which is probably what kept us afloat. It proved what I have always believed: There is enough.

———

PAJAMA PROGRAM'S FIRST real and necessary step to becoming official surfaced soon enough. All of my professional career, I was able to quickly understand and accomplish whatever next steps were necessary to get ahead. I had mentors, paid my dues, learned the ropes, and followed each new step to the next logical one. But now I found myself in very different waters. Nonprofit work is business, indeed, but it's a very different world. I knew none of the rules, and few of the players.

I figured an attorney needed to be involved, but I had to find the right one—one I could trust to keep this quiet and who wouldn't charge me an attorney's fee. One morning before I left the house,

I looked at Demo, raised my fist, and boldly announced, "I NEED TO FIND MY ATTORNEY."

He just smiled, as he often does. "Then go get one."

Later that morning, I got off the train, walked to my corner coffee guy for my daily brew, and waited on the corner for the light to change. Someone tapped me on my shoulder.

"Genevieve?" a dark-haired man said. "Remember me?"

I didn't.

"I'm Mary's friend, Santiago? We met a few years ago?"

Of course! I remembered Santiago! And I also remembered that he was an attorney! Let me tell you, fate can be a beautiful thing. So can a fist full of fortitude.

We set a time to catch up, and the next day into his office I walked. After two minutes of pleasantries, I told him I needed a free or dirt-cheap attorney. I told him why. Ever obliging, and ever understanding, Santiago gladly provided me with some names and numbers.

One of the attorneys was a lovely woman who said she'd be happy to meet with me. I was excited and nervous. Where to start? She told me about 501(c)(3)s and what I'd need to do to file as one. A 501(c)(3) from the US government would give us not only tax-free status, but legitimacy as a charity—it lets everyone know we have been vetted and that donations are tax deductible. I had to write up a mission for Pajama Program, collect some testimonials, prove there was a need, and list my board of directors.

Gulp. Wait . . . board of directors? How many?

"A minimum of three," she said.

OK, that was easy. I signed up me, Demo, and my friend Alice. Back in 2001, Alice and I started a side business. Alice designed beautiful one-of-a-kind hats while I did the marketing. Even though the business didn't succeed, our friendship flourished.

The attorney agreed to give us a discount rate, and I was happy to pay her. I received good advice from peers—pay a good professional, and you'll get good professional help. So I did.

One of the first things my new attorney said to me was "Why don't you consider 'piggy-backing' with another established nonprofit that you're already helping? It'll be a lot easier than filling out all these forms and trying to get your own 501(c)(3), trust me."

What? Give up the idea of Pajama Program as I believed it to be? As I dreamed it could be? What? Cast aside all my confidence and courage and simply join up with another charity to make it easier? At that moment, my eyes started to well up with tears and a knot formed in the pit of my stomach. The thought that we might be turned down, that Pajama Program wasn't good enough to stand alone, was devastating.

I couldn't wrap my mind around the possibility that I might not be able to move Pajama Program forward. Could I have made a mistake in running with this crazy idea? A mistake that would disappoint all these children? A mistake that could ruin my life? I could hardly catch my breath.

"No, we'll get our own 501(c)(3), thanks," I said to her. "They'll approve us."

And so, with Demo's help, I applied, and then waited and waited, continuing our deliveries and writing back to people asking us about our 501(c)(3) status to let them know we'd filled out the paperwork. The wait was downright agonizing.

There was still plenty to keep me busy, like coming up with a logo and brochures. Yikes! While I had forged a career in marketing, I had no artistic skills or experience with pitching anything outside a television rerun, so I adhered to the KISS (Keep It Simple, Stupid) approach.

The side business (Bella Luna) that I'd begun with my hat-designing friend and now fellow board member, Alice, had a crescent moon as its logo. Conveniently, the moon also worked for Pajama Program.

With zero art skills, I designed our first brochure on my computer. I figured out how to make three panels on a sheet that I could fold to look "professional." A little cut-and-paste, a little tweaking from more artistic people, and presto, it was done.

Meanwhile, people were constantly telling me, "Listen, Gen, the most important thing you need is a concise elevator speech."

Pardon?

"An elevator ride with a stranger. Think about it. You've got two minutes to pitch what you do and why it matters. You've got to totally nail that pitch."

What rolled off my tongue was this:

"We provide new pajamas and new books to children waiting and hoping to be adopted, and children in need." Clean, simple, and true.

What was my title? I had to look up nonprofit titles. Founder!

I was officially the founder and officially overwhelmed. Even with Demo's help, it was becoming too much for me to handle. I finally realized that I couldn't do it alone.

I knew what we needed was a real board of directors. But who fit the bill? I knew I had to focus my energy and intention on finding VIPs, people who worked with the children we served, some movers and shakers—individuals who could attract their friends to our cause. I was never one of those "ladies who lunch," a woman who could pick up the phone and get $10,000 in five minutes.

I couldn't think of anyone I knew who would fit the criteria of a true board member. I came to the conclusion that I'd have to ask perfect strangers. And perfect strangers could very possibly refuse me. Was I brave enough to ask?

My gut reaction was NO, I was not that brave. I was petrified. Wow, me, the woman who always jumped in first and figured it out later, the woman who had "feel the fear and do it anyway" seared into her brain, was afraid of failing so deeply that I didn't even recognize myself. But I knew why. This time and this fear were different.

I knew I was afraid because now I would be asking for the children, and I refused to be another person in the long line of people who disappointed them. Every day of their lives, they had their hopes dashed by someone who was supposed to be there for them, protect them, and love them. Now it was my turn. Would I be any different? Would I fail them, too? The thought made me sick to my stomach.

Even starting to imagine what or how I would ask for help made me quiver. I couldn't even form the question in my head, never mind asking it out loud. I knew that if people said no to me, I would fall apart, melting like the wicked witch in *The Wizard of Oz* right in front of them, and the embarrassment would be too much for me to handle. I would be a complete failure for these children and could never face them, or myself, again. How's that for fear? But I guess that's always the first question, isn't it, in any new venture: Are you brave enough? I'd have to be.

Fortunately, my fear wasn't running the whole show. I summoned up some moxie and remembered all the past magical occurrences that proved to me there had to be higher powers at work. I took a deep breath and looked for more.

Alice mentioned a few people she'd heard of who might know people "who knew the right people" in New York City. Before I gave it too much thought and scared myself out of the whole thing, I started making calls to every one of them.

After making my way through a long list, I reached a woman named Sharon. She took my call and seemed relatively interested, so we met for breakfast. Sharon wasn't exactly what I was expecting: A tiny lady with strawberry blond shoulder-length hair and bangs wearing a designer ivory-colored jacket with a fur collar. She wore a yellow diamond ring bigger than her finger, a diamond-encrusted necklace, and high heels, which made her all of five feet tall. My anxiety rose a notch.

I was very nervous at that first breakfast with Sharon, and I talked nonstop through egg-white omelets, toast, croissants, and cappuccinos.

Finally I put down my napkin, crossed my silverware over my plate, and took a breath. "So, you think you can help us?"

She nodded. "I'd be honored to."

Then she added, "I've got friends, too." And she winked.

I told Sharon I wanted to ask Jennefer, my PR friend, to join our board, and when I did ask her, it only took her seconds to say yes.

Sharon, Jennefer, and I agreed that we needed someone on our board who deeply knew the children we were serving and would make sure we were on track with our mission and activities. I looked up the Administration for Children's Services (ACS) in New York City and someone named Willie jumped up off the list at me. His title indicated that he worked directly with the children, so in my mind he was our guy. I cold-called him and explained, in my best elevator pitch, how my board and I had started Pajama Program, and we wanted to meet with him about our mission and his kids.

"OK," he said, "come on in."

Sharon and I marched into Willie's office at the ACS shelter with no script, just determination and smiles. We met Willie, who at more than six feet tall hovered over us and had a zealous handshake that welcomed us to his world. I mustered my courage and sprang into our very bold request: "We want the children coming into your citywide shelter for the first time to have new, warm pajamas and new books for bedtime. And in time, we want to set up a schedule to come in and read with them in the evenings so they know we care, and that they're cared for. And we'd like you to join our board of directors."

We didn't beat around any bushes that day, let me tell you.

Sharon and I went on about our plans, about where we saw the program going, why it was so critical, how necessary it was for the children of New York's shelters. We appeared to have a premeditated plan, but truthfully, we were just speaking from the heart. Sometimes, speaking from the heart is all that matters.

"Sounds great to me," said Willie. "Send the pajamas and books. And yes, I'll gladly be on your board."

Sharon and I looked at each other in delight.

Willie was energized from the get-go. What spirit he had! And yet, over the next few weeks we were all surprised and a bit worried when his bosses told him that they had to investigate Pajama Program and Willie's potential role. It seemed that an individual at ACS couldn't agree to join a nonprofit board without abiding by certain procedures and rules.

Still, we kept bringing him pajamas and books for the children in his program, and ultimately, Willie and his superiors grew convinced that our intentions were authentic. Thankfully, he stuck it out through the vetting process, and finally, he was cleared to join us as a board member.

To this day, Willie tells people about the moment that "two ladies I'd never met came into my office, plopped themselves down in front of me, and proceeded to tell me that the children needed pajamas and books or they would have nightmares. All through their pitch I kept thinking, 'Yeah, we'll see if they come through with any of this!' I'm here to tell you right now that those two ladies came through."

One morning, a beautiful woman in her forties came into the retail store of my importing business client. (When they needed me to work retail, I was happy to.) The woman was smart, elegant, and very personable. I helped her find what she needed and checked her out at the register. Her name was Paula, she was a physician, and she lived on the Upper East Side. "Wow," I thought, as I helped her pack all her new purchases into the bags, "it must be so nice to have gorgeous, soft sheets on your bed every night." I thought of the children we knew, and I thought about their beds. Paula had means, that was clear, but most importantly, she had a compassionate and thoughtful way about her. She was the kind of person we needed on our board, too.

And yet, I didn't have the nerve to say, "Excuse me, you are so poised and lovely, would you like to be on the board of my nonprofit no one knows about and I have absolutely no experience running?"

I kicked myself all morning for not even attempting to ask her. I didn't think my boss would approve, but maybe I should have struck up a conversation and made my request. But I hadn't.

It was a missed opportunity. I figured my chance with Paula had come and gone, and that was that. Later that afternoon, however, I noticed that my thin gold watch was no longer on my left wrist. I didn't have many precious items of jewelry, so the watch was very special to me. I racked my brain thinking of what could have happened to it. "Oh no," I thought, "maybe while I was helping Paula with her sheets it came loose and dropped into one of her bags."

I looked up her information and realized she gave us her office address and number, so I called. Paula's assistant answered, and I told her my plight. She said she'd get back to me. That evening Paula called me personally.

"Genevieve, I have your pretty watch!" she said. "Would you like to come and get it tomorrow?"

I told her I would. I'm sure she thought my excitement was about my watch, while I knew it was partly about my watch and partly about another chance to ask her the big question.

When I met her the next day, I thanked her for getting my watch back to me and blurted out something like "Listen, I'm starting a nonprofit . . . [insert elevator speech] . . . and I would love it if you would consider a place on our board."

I'm nothing if not determined.

"That sounds lovely," she replied graciously. "Why yes, I'd love to!"

I stifled the urge to fall over, but I managed instead to stay upright and say, with the utmost composure, "How nice of you! I will give you a call next week."

I left convinced she thought I asked people this all the time.

Ours was not a traditional board of directors, filled with business-people chosen because of our needs and their strengths. That would come later. This initial board grew out of emotions and sensibilities. That's what we were at the beginning: one big beating heart.

Our first board project was a simple purse party! We hoped to raise money and attract donors and volunteers. We invited a small group of women for a night of wine, cheese, and purses for sale. Sharon's friend had a connection to an importer of beautiful leather handbags who gave them to us on consignment for our fundraiser.

On the afternoon of the party, I met the mailman in our lobby. I hurriedly scanned the envelopes and saw a thin letter from the IRS. I started to sweat. Open it or not? Feel the fear and do it any-way, one of my mantras. Scanning it quickly, I saw only one word:

APPROVED! I was so excited I could have run all the way into Manhattan. But Demo was waiting outside in the car, so as I opened the car door with a huge smile, I held the letter to my chest and said, "Our 501(c)(3) was approved!"

That evening, I headed to the purse event, thrilled with the knowledge that we were official! The party turned out to be a hit—chatty and fun, just like we'd hoped. And we made some money. The whole thing was exhilarating. We were on our way. First up was replying to those letters from potential donors asking about our 501(c)(3) status.

———

WITH OUR PAPERWORK in hand, I knew something would have to give regarding my part-time job. Was I going to quit or was I going to be fired? The company was hanging in there, and I thought I would, too.

Demo knew I was fighting a harsh inner battle between Pajama Program and my job. You can imagine my shock when he said, "Quit your job, I got you." Now that's love. Through all our ups and downs, my selfish acts and tunnel vision, the countless anxiety attacks he babysat me through, and my financial fibs galore, it turned out Demo was the strong one. We had a connection that couldn't be broken.

I felt very strange that first evening I walked into our apartment having quit my job. I felt out of sorts and weird, like out of my body surreal. And that did a number on my head. All this pajama stuff became real, very real. And real was now really scary. I was no longer my usual responsible, sensible, confident self. Gone was the familiar feeling that I knew what I was doing and that I could easily find my place in any scenario. Uncertainty filled me. I had to force myself not to worry. I couldn't tell Demo I had my doubts, not after pretending all would be just fine.

To regain my footing, I started creating to-do lists in my head and thought about my number one priority: crafting a strong and concise description of Pajama Program. This was as much for me as it was for everyone else I invited into my strange new world. I wasn't relieved about having "free time" to do this, because it wasn't like I was retiring with money to spend . . . or leaving my job for a better one. I knew I was taking a humongous leap of faith, and maybe it was the stupidest and most irresponsible thing I had ever done. Or maybe, with the horizon full of opportunity and my ability to make choices every day, it was the best decision of my life.

I jumped off the cliff and kept looking up.

The Heart of the Matter

- Feel the fear and do it anyway.

ANY MAJOR LEAP takes courage, faith, and an ability to train yourself to look up when your instinct is to look down. Whether you jump off the corporate ladder, change your life in another way, or simply make a commitment to try something new, fear will creep into your brain and your body. If your heart is crystal clear, put it in the driver's seat. Your brain will figure out how to make peace with it and help you thrive under these new circumstances. But expect nothing to be the same. You, your relationships, and your work will be transformed. And transformation can lead to more fulfillment . . . for everyone involved.

- Embrace the human connection . . . again and again!

FINDING A SUPPORTIVE network, like a dedicated board of directors, is a mix of serendipitous meetings, a steadfast intention to attract the right people, and a dose of moxie or two! In most instances, face-to-face engagement compelled people to join in the cause. What I felt that night with the little girl transferred to many others through some sort of osmosis. Yes, putting yourself on the line in front of people can be daunting. Trust in the human connection to lead you to the people who are looking for someone like you!

- Every day we have a choice.

MOST OF US forget that fact—and it is a fact. When you open your eyes every morning, you can consciously make a choice: Same path as yesterday or different? There's no law that says once you change course, you can't go back. I took solace in remembering that. Every day, I had a choice. Keep going or turn back. It's always up to you.

Chapter 9

You're Either a Looker
or a Leaper

Shortly after leaving the workforce, I was still looking up—up at the ceiling, unable to sleep. It was about 2 a.m. when Demo roused to see me pacing the bedroom floor, fraught with anxieties, muttering to myself, "Are we doing enough?"

I somehow fell asleep and was awakened by Demo handing me a cup of green tea along with something he had written longhand on a piece of notebook paper. As I read it, I could only whisper, "How did you know?"

"I see you living it," he replied, and clinked his cup to mine. "Everyone needs a mission statement, Gen. Now maybe you and Pajama Program have yours."

For the Children

We shall walk, hand in hand, the pathways of light to reach the children who have been neglected, orphaned, and abandoned.

We shall be the inspiration to uplift their heavy hearts and foster the smile of hope that they so rightly deserve to wear upon their precious faces.

We shall read them marvelous stories to expand their imagination and return the wonder to their eyes.

We shall nurture their hearts with caring, open their minds with books, and comfort them with warm cozy pajamas for bedtime to lessen their dreaded fear of not belonging.

We shall encourage them to dream their dreams filled with desire and the magic of possibilities.

We shall take comfort in knowing that we have touched the children deeply, tendered their gentle souls, and sown the seeds of love that they so desperately needed.

We will be filled with an inexplicable joy knowing that in giving we truly made a difference. And when the sun sets upon our mission, we will all have moved together through the darkness and awakened to a brighter day.

And on that day, the children will belong to themselves, walking hand in hand as one with us on the pathways of light, reaching out to the neglected, the orphaned, and the abandoned.

———

WE ALL NEED a mission statement that inspires us. It should be personal, something that resonates with our heart and brings us back to our path when doubts and fears pull us off center. It also has to be put in a place where we see it every day.

I put Demo's mission statement on my dresser, where I could see it every morning and night. And boy, did I need it during what proved to be a very difficult change. Month to month, Demo and I weren't sure how we'd survive financially.

Donations were coming in, and I was learning the fine art of grant writing. The real "art" I discovered is the six degrees of separation rule. Most of the donations were from friends of friends, and friends in companies with budgets for community giving. I knew the flow was too slow and we had to find a way to bring in the big bucks. Or at least some bigger bucks.

Demo and I had a very limited budget, tight living quarters, raw nerves, overbooked schedules, and no downtime. Added to all that stress was the fact that we had only one car between us. I was convinced there would be trouble ahead.

There was absolutely no way we could afford a second car, not even a cheap one, so we set out to literally map out the days and weeks ahead. Just the pajama and book pick-ups and the deliveries filled every month's calendar, and that wasn't adding Demo into the equation. But for me, there was no alternative but to push through

my to-do list. And once Demo saw my unrelenting determination—which I hoped was one of the very reasons he'd fallen in love
with me—was here to stay, we sighed together, cried together, and
then rolled up our sleeves together.

I'll never forget the day Demo showed me several pages of blank
paper he had taped together and said, "This is our car schedule." He
had written the days of the week for the next month at the top of
the pages, and under each day, he broke down by the hour which
of us had the car alone for our own use and the hours we had it
together for Pajama Program. I was so touched I would have married him all over again right then.

With Demo's help, the planets aligned every time, and we were
able to successfully share the car and get our work accomplished. I
was beginning to see that things were falling into place easier than
ever before. Sometimes, it felt a little spooky when all of a sudden
events shifted to make possible what had been impossible an hour
before. Once when I overloaded an entire week's schedule and realized I could never make all the deliveries I promised, nearly half
of the places so grateful for pajamas and books called to ask if they
could pick up the gifts from me so I wouldn't have to go out of my
way! I held my breath not to jinx my good fortune. Often it felt like
an invisible force was working to help me whenever I couldn't find
a way. These coincidences gave me the courage to believe I was on
track with my purpose. And that was good because we had some
serious work to do.

Demo and I stayed strong and committed, but we also argued,
mostly about money. Financial concerns have a way of doing that
to even the healthiest couples. Demo never wavered in his support,
but I know I tested his patience.

Of course, I knew that conventional wisdom would not have

told me to completely overhaul my life when I was 38. I was aware that the most comfortable way to operate in the world would've been to keep moving forward with my career, make more money, and retire with a healthy bank account so I could live the life I'd planned on and worked so hard for. That's what my brain would tell me. But my heart? Well, let's just say my heart can beat pretty loud.

The victorious purse party gave us the confidence to go for something bigger.

"Let's have a gala luncheon," Sharon suggested. "We'll book the Plaza Athénée ballroom. We'll get sponsors, sell tables and tickets, have celebrity honorees, and it will be a terrific fundraiser for Pajama Program and put us on the map in NYC."

My first thought was "Is she kidding? What celebrities will let us honor them? Who in the world will buy a $250 ticket, much less a whole table? And who the heck is going to pay for the Plaza Athénée?" Miraculously, I managed to keep the astonished expression off my face and responded in my usual I-do-this-all-the-time manner, saying, "Great idea, where do we start?"

Well, let me tell you, Sharon had some friends back then— among them, Mercedes Ellington (Duke's granddaughter), Ivana Trump, and Dylan Lauren (Ralph's daughter). Dylan, who owned Dylan's Candy Bar, was more of a neighborly acquaintance, but to Sharon, if she repeatedly saw the same person in her neighborhood, she considered them a close personal friend, and she had no trouble asking them for favors.

Sharon asked Mercedes if she would take part since she taught dance to at-risk teens, and she accepted. The next time Sharon saw Dylan on Lexington Avenue, she struck up a conversation about all the parties Dylan did for shelter children and then asked her to be part of our luncheon program, too. Lo and behold, Dylan agreed, as did Ivana, who was raising her young children as best she could during a difficult divorce.

Now to fill the room . . . or at least make it not look embarrassingly empty.

I am not a particularly well-connected person, as I have said. I am not a genius, nor am I a math whiz. What I am, crazy or not, is someone who has a lot of trust in the "jump in the water and splash around until you are swimming" philosophy, so any doubts weren't going to stop me from trying to throw the world's best luncheon with a little profit after expenses. We made invitations and mailed them with a kiss and a prayer, literally. We sold 67 tickets. Sharon, Jennefer, and Paula sold 65 and I sold two. That was about 66 more people than I thought would come. Jennefer got some press for us in small local neighborhood papers, and we were on our way to making some noise!

Smarter people will look before they leap. Not me. I'm a leaper. But as our gala date got closer, I was terrified. Fundraising, I knew, was the key to staying afloat. Without a stockpile of funds, and then a steady stream of donations and more fundraising events, we could sink. We needed to keep our Pajama boat afloat.

In order to try and relax ahead of our big luncheon, Demo and I started to take long walks in a nearby park. We sat on benches, daydreaming. Demo's favorite topic was Oprah, and he was always trying to get me to focus on this one dream: getting Pajama Program to her. He believed she was the one person who could help me tell so many others about these children and our work. He knew she understood "finding your purpose" and that she'd want to help if she only heard about us! Demo would be calm, reassuring, even funny, and I would be stressed, worried, and excited, all the while talking OPRAH.

While these bench-breaks with Demo helped me relax for short periods, I still felt the full weight of our upcoming luncheon fundraiser on my shoulders. I had to continually find ways to absorb the pain I felt for all the children on our list while I grappled with fundraising and our growing "Needs Pajamas" list.

The day of our luncheon arrived and there was a buzz in the room. I know many of our guests were wondering what this Pajama Program was all about. Willie took the reins. He stood up and told everyone how important our work was for the children he looked after every night, how police are forced to remove them from horrific home situations, and how frightened the children are when they first enter the shelter. It was all he could do to keep it together, and his voice cracked as he told us stories about the boys and girls he knew. The room was silent.

Every guest was engaged and emotional. Ralph Lauren's wife, Ricky, came to support Dylan and spoke about how much she loved hearing about Pajama Program. She said she would tell everyone she knew about our work.

Suddenly, the buzz in the room electrified—the galvanized charge of a group of people understanding that they could do good, authentic good, felt tangible. It was the human connection in all its glory! Demo was beside me, and I glanced over at him. We both knew this was going to catch on.

After the gala luncheon, we were on a roll, and I was beginning to feel fearless! New supporters were coming forward and Sharon, Jennefer, Willie, Paula, and I were making plans to engage them further. We reveled in the notion of a rock-solid future, one with real possibilities, genuine prospects, and a bona fide path for making a difference to these children. Maybe I'd even find a way to get some sound sleep.

A couple of months into the new year, Demo and I took a break and went to a movie one Saturday afternoon. We purchased our tickets and on the way to the popcorn line, I nudged Demo.

"Hey, isn't that Meredith Vieira over there in line? I think those are her kids with her. Remember I told you I watch her on *The View* all the time, and she'd be a GREAT Mother of the Year for us? Remember?!" I said, thinking about our next fundraiser.

"Yes, yes, I remember. That's definitely her," he said. "Go ask her."

"Go ask her?!" I wavered. My fearlessness was betraying me. I stood stiff as a statue, staring at her. She laughed with her youngest and right then I felt her love. Then something inside me kicked in, or maybe just kicked me, and I found my courage. I walked over to her with shaky legs, which I hoped she didn't notice.

"Ms. Vieira, I don't want to bother you, but I'm the founder of Pajama Program and we give pajamas and books to children in need, and I think you would make a terrific Mother of the Year," I blurted out. "May we honor you in May?"

I could tell she liked what I said. Her lips curled up in a tender and sweet smile.

"Oh, that's so nice!" she said. "Let me give you my assistant's phone number. Give her a call, and let's see."

We called, and then waited. And waited. As the date for what would become an annual benefit for us crept closer without an honoree, I prayed every time my phone rang that it was WABC-TV calling. And one day it was. In May 2004, we honored Meredith Vieira, and for many years that followed, she was the narrator of our Pajama Program presentation video.

———

THINGS WERE INSANE with my trying to run the mounting administrative part of Pajama Program from our apartment, where Demo also was trying to work. The fact that Demo was often on his computer in between acting jobs didn't stop me from recruiting him every day, all day, to help me. Of course, I thought what I was doing was more important than what he was doing.

Life behind the scenes after our first two big fundraising events was pretty much the same, but it looked different to the outside world. To our guests and new supporters, we were legitimate. But to those of us in the know, we felt more pressure than ever, despite the exhilaration. Having our 501(c)(3) helped us attract more supporters, and we were able to fill out corporate and foundation grant applications through their connections. We knew that there were a lot more eyeballs on us.

Demo's good friend David, an award-winning architect, doting husband, and inspiring father, loved Pajama Program and knew how crowded and hectic things were in our little love nest. Ha! One day, he called to offer me a work cubicle at his firm until he hired another employee.

It was one of those moments when you think, is there a catch here? I'm sure he means for a couple of weeks, no longer than that.

I was both beyond excited and scared to death. This was a sign that someone else was taking a chance on me—*me*, someone who was shooting from the hip with lots of prayers along the way, every day. David believed in me, and I felt humbled.

"Thank you so much" was all I could muster.

David saved the day—and probably our marriage—with his offer. I took my computer and off I went to his office on East 27th Street. This space was just what I needed to administer Pajama Program—a part of my job that was growing very fast. Our Yonkers Reading Center was just enough space for me to read with children in the afternoons and evenings and where kind strangers could drop off pajamas to be organized later. But with this newfound space, I was really able to separate Pajama Program from my personal life—what was left of it! I could leave Demo alone at home to work in peace.

The cubicle was a godsend for me, but I'm not sure it was for David's employees. Every morning and afternoon in my little cubicle, I repeatedly opened and emptied boxes of pajamas, then counted and sorted them all into new boxes, which then had to be taped shut. The tape gun screeched like nails on a chalkboard. And I took phone calls all day, which everyone on the floor could hear. Shelter staff were telling their friends about the lady giving pajamas to kids in shelters, and calls were coming in from states as far away as Illinois and Texas. It was me, Demo, Ana, Geri, and volunteers I had never met all working together as a team.

The pile of boxes flowed out of my new cubicle space into every hallway, growing higher and higher from 9 a.m. to 5 p.m. Impatiently, I waited for Mr. UPS to come pick them up to take them as far away as Washington state and every state in between, thanks to *Parenting* magazine readers and 34 Pajama Program chapters.

I realized I could use a lot more help, at least another body, so I put an ad on Craigslist for a volunteer a couple of days a week. I figured the volunteer could work on the computer in the cubicle on days when I was out making deliveries.

My ad went up, and immediately I got replies. I read each letter and resume, but one in particular got my attention. I really don't know why I was fixated on this letter and resume from a woman named Terri. Her letter said she had recently moved to New York from Seattle and was intrigued by my program.

On paper, Terri looked professional, mature, and definitely experienced as a past board member of multiple nonprofits. But there was something else—my gut feeling. As I read her resume, I felt a surge of excitement and confidence. I had to meet her.

I called Terri and set up a meeting for the next day, ignoring all the other replies to my ad. We met at a breakfast place in Grand Central and chatted. She was almost 50 years old, had had a career in the food business in Seattle, and really wanted to work in the food industry in New York. She told me about her disappointing interviews (she sensed they thought she was too old to be hired). She'd served on nonprofit boards in the past and was interested in finding out what I was trying to build. I immediately knew she was perfect.

I didn't pick Terri because of any similarities between us. In fact, we were opposites across the board. Until arriving in New York, Terri had spent her life in Indiana and Seattle; I was a New Yorker through and through. She would one day soon become a grandmother; I'd never had children. Terri dressed casually, and I was always dressed for a party. She was cautious, I could tell, and I jumped into the water first and then splashed around, hoping to float!

Maybe those were the exact reasons I knew Terri was the one. Plus, she loved food, and I loved food. And that's a pretty powerful bond for me! We got along really well, and after about 30 minutes, she asked me, "So what's your process for making your decision on whom to pick, and why can't you pay?"

"I've made my decision," I told her. "I want you, so it's up to you. I can't pay you yet, but I promise I will. Call me, and let me know if you're interested." She called the next day and accepted.

Terri and I made a schedule to share the week in the cubicle. I told her everything I was doing, and she was on board.

———

AROUND THE TIME I hired Terri, I was canvassing Westchester (a suburb north of New York City) for Pajama Program support, and someone told me about a successful businessman named Randy Weis who ran a local flooring company called RD Weis. I left a voice mail for Randy saying something like "I'm the founder of Pajama Program, and we have our first Reading Center in Yonkers for Westchester kids, and I'd love to talk to you."

Randy called back at 6:30 p.m., and the next morning at 8 a.m. sharp, we met in his office. Randy was easy to be with. A man of style—in dress, office décor, and with people. Not only did he invite me in warmly, I could tell he cared about his employees. He was kind to those few who interrupted our meeting, and he introduced me to them all.

Randy didn't waste any time. "Other than funds, what else do you need?" he asked me.

"A VAN! I'm sharing a car, and it's just impossible to stuff all the pajamas and books in it," I said. "I have to make pick-ups every day . . . and deliveries to the kids all over this county . . . and everything is getting mixed up because I don't have enough room in the trunk and backseat . . . I have my materials, and they're getting ruined . . ." I rambled on.

He listened patiently. When I finally shut up, he said, "Maybe I can help with that!"

Randy had acquired a few pre-owned vehicles when he merged with another company. Magically, he produced a Pajama Program van, a supersized, sparkling white van, with lots of space for boxes and bags. He even carpeted the inside in a bright blue, and before he delivered it, he called in favors and had our Pajama Program logos painted on the side! I could tell already, this Randy man had wings!

The Heart of the Matter

* No more playing small.

THE SIMPLE ACT of making your decision to grow will call into play everything you've learned already on your purpose journey: Trust that the universe will align the planets and the human connection will move people. Lead with meaning, and what you need will manifest at the right time. Oh, and remember, you will feel fear, but just do it anyway.

For us, the act of making the decision to take Pajama Program to the next level seemed to give us remarkable power. Successful fundraising benefits, the gift of a van, a welcoming office space, the perfect assistant, and a chance meeting in a movie theater all manifested in astonishing ways to elevate our game and serve more children.

Chapter 10

One Flip-Flop
and a Hurricane

*N*ever could I have imagined that Pajama Program was about to be challenged in a bigger way than I could imagine. Thank God that David's cubicle and Terri and Randy entered my life when they did, because I would need all the resources and help I could get for what lay around the corner—1,200 miles away.

Hurricane Katrina hit the Gulf Coast on August 23, 2005. Along with the rest of the country, we watched the horror of the storm on television: houses being washed away, cars sinking, people climbing trees for safety, families floating in makeshift canoes, children abandoned, pets needing to be rescued.

"How do we get pajamas to those kids in Louisiana?" Randy asked me. "They're busing them all to the Houston Astrodome with nothing but a Tupperware box to hold whatever they could get before they evacuated. Gen, I'll provide the truck and drivers if you can fill it. Use my address as a loading dock, and have people send pajamas here."

And that's what we did. Emails galore went out to everyone—friends of friends were getting in on our mission. Hundreds of people were spreading the word about the "truck of pajamas for Katrina kids." Out of the blue, CBS News called and said they'd heard about our trip and wanted me to come in at the crack of dawn to be on their morning show before we headed south. I was thrilled, of course, but with all the logistical uncertainty, I was nervous. We had sheer determination and will but not a confirmed way to get to the children directly. I went on the show and explained Pajama Program and our intentions and discussed how many people were sending us pajamas for our truck in response to our emails asking, begging, for help. As a result of the morning news spot, Randy's loading dock was never busier with FedEx packages, UPS boxes, and people coming by with bags of pajamas. Every day, the box truck got fuller.

Our destination was the Houston Astrodome. People helping us put everything in order were working on a contact in Houston to provide us access to the families in the 'Dome—and give their children warm pajamas. We could see on TV that they were wearing the same clothes for several days and nights already. So far, we didn't have an "in" to deliver our gifts to the children, but we intended to find a way.

I couldn't fit in the truck with the driver and the two helpers Randy put on the job. Terri had just started with Pajama Program and was instantly a godsend. She immediately volunteered to give me frequent flier miles to fly to Houston! I knew when I met her she was a very special lady, but now I knew Terri would be one of my soulmates. Sharon got me a free room in a timeshare club where her friend was a member, so I was set.

In Houston, a pediatric nurse named Lin had become my new BFF through the week of preparations. I found her through a long link of referrals, and she "got it" when I told her what we were planning. We spoke several times about my trip and our supply of pajamas. She was encouraging and as confident as we were that we'd make our way to the children.

"These children have nothing, and they are afraid," she said. "Their parents are trying to keep it together, but they're at their wit's end and they've lost *everything*. None of them have slept a wink for days here. Not only are they petrified and in shock, they are afraid others will take the little they have in their Tupperware boxes."

Nothing was going to stop us after hearing that.

Our truck left early on Sunday morning with Carlos, the driver, and Melissa and Andre, volunteers from Randy's company. I was flying in the next morning. Sunday midday I got a call from Randy. "The truck broke down," he said. "They're in PA, and we're trying to find a mechanic."

My heart sank. I waited. I knew Randy would stop at nothing to get the truck going again, so I waited and waited for the next call. Randy called again a couple of hours later.

"They found the only garage in town, but it's closed so I called the local police there, told them what's in the truck and where it's going, and begged him to find the owner of the garage. I'm waiting for a call."

Minutes, then hours passed, and finally Randy called me again. "They found the mechanic, and he's on the way to open his garage and see if he can fix the truck. My guys are anxious to get back on the road, and they've been troupers—there's no AC in that truck, and it's a long drive to Texas!"

I breathed a sigh of relief. I knew Randy would find a way—I knew he had magic.

The truck was again on its way late Sunday, and the ETA to meet me in Houston was Monday evening.

I waited all Monday, checking in with phone calls to the drivers, looking for contacts at the Astrodome, talking to Lin to see if she was faring any better than I was at getting us permission to give out all our pajamas. There was no news yet. Lin had been trying to get herself into the Astrodome to help. Security was incredibly tight, and I was sure they were skeptical of us and our truck, but I knew Lin was our key into that giant arena. I knew she would find a way—I knew she had magic, too.

Carlos called me at 11:45 p.m. that night. They had just pulled onto the street leading to the Astrodome. "What do we do?" he asked me.

"Head over there, and I will call you right back."

I called Lin.

"I'm in," she said, "and I'm helping the doctors and tending to the children. Are you coming?"

"Our truck is headed to the Astrodome, and I'm standing outside," I told her.

"Go to the load-in door. Call me when the truck is there."

I saw the truck coming down the street. It was pitch black with just a few streetlights. There was not a soul in sight. One uptight security guard was nearby, guarding the door and watching me, confident I was going to cause a problem, and just waiting for the right moment to ask me what the heck was going on. As he came closer, I waved the truck to get as close to me and the giant dock door as possible.

"Hey, what are you doing?" the guard yelled at me. I ignored him and hit redial.

"Lin, we are all here right at the big door. Help!"

Through the sliver of space between the double entry doors, I heard her tell the guard inside to open the door for her.

"What are you talking about?" I heard him ask her sarcastically.

"Just open this door NOW!" she reprimanded him. She meant business.

"There is a truck out there with pajamas for the children and babies in here, and they need this stuff immediately. They need clean clothes now, so open this door!"

Apparently, he wasn't convinced.

Lin yelled louder, "DO YOU SEE THESE CHILDREN???" (I imagined her making him look at them all.) "I said open this door now, or I will get the doctors and police here and tell them that you are keeping these children in unsafe health conditions with help available to them right outside this door!"

We heard some mechanical grumbling and held our breath as we saw the giant door slowly and heavily open to reveal the floor of the Astrodome. As silent as it was outside, it was even quieter in that huge sports arena. All we saw were rows and rows of cots with large Tupperware boxes at the side of each one. People were lying or sitting on the beds. Those awake were speaking in hushed tones, eyes now peering our way. It was unnerving how still it was inside.

"Drive that truck in here slowly," Lin instructed Carlos. And he did, very slowly.

The truck came to a halt. Carlos, Melissa, Andre, and I huddled with Lin to make a plan. Melissa and I feared people would storm the vehicle, mothers and fathers desperate for something for their children. But there was no rush of a mob, no uncontrollable crowd, just curious and weary faces staring at us.

Quietly, the five of us approached the closest families and told them what we had. We brought the families to the truck and started to hand them pajamas and a few other supplies we had, including diapers. They were so grateful and polite, almost timid in taking the gifts. We knew how much they needed them.

In small groups, families came up to the truck, and we handed out that first load—more than 5,000 pajamas. In the next few hours, we met thousands of families, hugged them all, and saw gratitude and hope in their eyes. Yes, it was about giving pajamas to the children, but it was also about the love that was being delivered to the mothers and fathers desperate to give their children comfort in an unimaginable situation. The pajamas were just the carriers of that love, delivered by a vehicle that rolled onto the floor of the convention center that late, late night.

Standing next to an empty baby stroller was a little boy, about seven years old. His mom was a few feet away with a baby at a makeshift information center waiting to fill out paperwork. I walked over and said hello to him. He had on white shorts and a blue T-shirt with a funny character on it. His nose was running, and I saw his knees were scraped. And then I realized something odd about his feet. He was wearing only one flip-flop; his other foot was bare. He saw me staring.

"I could only find one," he told me.

"Would you like a pair of pajamas?" I asked him.

"Yes, please," he said. I gave him two pairs—one with dinosaurs on it and one camouflage print.

To this day, I wish I'd asked him his name. The little boy with one flip-flop took the pajamas and hung them on the handle of the baby carriage. He flashed me a titanic smile, and then gave me two thumbs up. If I didn't know where I was, I would've sworn I was at his little league game where he'd just hit a home run!

The promise of hope—that's what this boy had. Stuck in the

midst of this dreadful turmoil, spinning through this devastating labyrinth that we all watched from afar, he believed the promise we made him—the promise that he was not forgotten. He and everyone else in that stadium, on that floor, on those cots, were in our hearts and minds every day. And a simple pair of pajamas was all he needed to feel our promise. We were connected in spirit, through love. He'd find hope on the other end of this tragedy. He believed it, and so did Carlos, Melissa, Andre, Randy, and I.

We ended up making two trips south, delivering a total of 11,000 pajamas for the children of Katrina. The experience is best captured in the first email I wrote to all our supporters who helped fill the first truck with pajamas:

Dear Friends,

The children have their pajamas now . . .

Last night, thousands and thousands of children sleeping on the Convention Center floor in Houston were sleeping in their first pair of pajamas in two weeks. And that's thanks to those of you who helped us fill our Pajama Program truck with more than 5,000 pajamas for the children of Hurricane Katrina, a catastrophe that has changed our lives forever.

Leaving Houston was very difficult. People are still in a daze, still frightened, still unsure of tomorrow. It hurts to look at them, and you can't tell them you understand . . . because you can't imagine it. How would you feel if everything you had was washed away and you and your family were on a blow-up mattress in a sea of blow-up mattresses trying to hide whatever you had accumulated in 12 days? It looked like a scene from a TV show about something that could happen at the end of the world.

When I started handing out pajamas to children in need four years ago, I wanted to hand out love and compassion with each pair, to let each child know someone cared. Never could I have imagined we would ever have to do what we did over the past 3 days . . . hand pajamas to children and families who had nothing left. I held back my tears every time I said, "Hello, what size does your child wear?" In addition to handing out our pajamas on the floor of the Convention Center, we visited seven shelters. It was so hard to watch the evacuees rummage through some things that are barely wearable to find anything. One man held a little boy by the hand and said to me, "My boy needs shoes." The boy was barefoot. I swallowed hard and took him to find a box I had seen of slightly worn children's shoes. Later, as the man walked out, he said to me, "My boy likes these." And he wore very cute sneakers and a big smile on his face. I cried. Gratifying, yes. Heartbreaking, definitely.

I sat with a 10-year-old boy named Carlton who had found an old game to play with while his mother went through the boxes for clothes for him and her. He wore sunglasses, and I teased him about it because we were inside. He grinned and said, "Something's wrong with my eye." He removed his sunglasses, and one eye was swollen and he had to keep the light out.

Owner Charlene of Houston-based PJ manufacturer Greggy Girl met me one of the mornings, and together with her caravan of volunteers and the 300-plus pajamas they donated, we spent the morning meeting evacuee children who were in schools so foreign to them. We met beautiful children who were just trying to fit in, into a new neighborhood, a new town—temporarily.

A personal thank-you goes to the staff and volunteers of the University of Texas Medical Center who early on asked for their headquarters at the Convention Center to be our focus with the pajama delivery. It is this group of dedicated and compassionate people who knew they needed what we had and made sure we were able to get it directly into the hands of the little ones. It was one nurse named Lin who runs pediatrics there who stood up to one man who thought our truck should not be on their floor—to tell him that these children need clean pajamas TONIGHT—they had waited too long for so little. The spirit of the American people is enormous and has been given new life, ironically, through Katrina. We should all be proud of how the people of Houston—and beyond—have banded together to help their neighbors. Theirs is a story to be told when this is all said and done.

As we walked away from the scene on the Convention floor we turned back one more time . . . with hope that they will find the strength to move forward. A special thank-you to Randy Weis for his words "Gen, I'll provide the truck and drivers if you can fill it."

We've now begun loading a second truck for delivery of pajamas for the children in Louisiana.

With deep gratitude and appreciation,
Genevieve

The Heart of the Matter

* You're not alone.

THERE ARE TIMES when it's physically, emotionally, and financially impossible to go it alone. And you'll find you don't have to when you are serving more than just your own needs. The Hurricane Katrina tragedy taught us a lesson on how to invite others—or, in a rare case like the one at that convention hall door, DEMAND others—to get on board for the greater good! A human connection domino effect was set in motion by Randy's call. When you're faced with moving a mountain, assemble a team and trust others will join in. You'll witness firsthand how fast the human connection comes to your aid. We connectors love to rally!

Chapter 11

Feeling the Pictures

$\mathcal{A}$fter 12 months in David's cubicle, he reluctantly broke the news to us that soon he would need our space for a new hire. His cubicle gift had been a game-changer. We felt legitimized and independent, and we were getting stronger every day. It was the spring of 2006, and Pajama Program had been official for five years, with me officially running it full-time for the last two. Now Pajama Program was about to be homeless.

Desperately trying to stay calm, Terri and I racked our brains for another working space to occupy for free. I did what I was becoming very accustomed to doing—I started calling strangers. How the name Regus came to mind I don't remember. Somehow the UK-based workspace provider got on my "potentially generous landlords" list. I faxed them about our plight. (We still faxed in those days!) Do you know, the next morning someone from their office called and set up a meeting for Terri and me with the manager of their beautiful space on Park Avenue in New York City, who promptly donated a small office to us. We couldn't believe our luck. It was a little bit of tenacity on my part, and a big lesson learned for "the universe is your partner" file. Yes, the universe deals in office space, too. We worked and thrived there for the next 12 months.

That May, we had the incredible fortune of honoring superstar Patti LaBelle at our annual fundraiser. We chose Ms. LaBelle because her story of raising her sisters' children was extraordinary. She was another of Sharon's six-degrees-of-separation connections. Ms. LaBelle had never heard of Pajama Program, but when she sat among all of us at that year's luncheon, listening to stories about our children and our journey, she felt compelled to disregard her manager's instructions not to sing.

"I'm loving this today," she said, "and I'm gonna sing."

Soulfully, she sang the Lord's Prayer a cappella. Not a single person made a sound, moved, or even twitched, and as she hit the final note, everyone in the room jumped to their feet and exploded in wild applause and cheers. I looked around and saw tears running down many of their faces.

We'd come a long way, but little did I know that soon a friend walking the beach with me would pose a little question and, along with it, a mind-blowing answer to boost us even further.

Demo and Claudia had been dear friends for more than 20 years, and they shared a lot of spiritual practices and impassioned discussions. Claudia is elegant and stylish, and she has a heart of gold. Every summer, we secretly hoped we'd get an invitation to her luxurious beach house on Long Island. On one such lucky summer day during a long walk together along the beach, Claudia listened intently to my Pajama Program updates on our new Reading Center in Yonkers, our work to attract more financial support, and my new "no-job, full-time Pajama Program status."

Then she stunned me.

"Genevieve, wouldn't you like a Reading Center in New York City, too?"

"Sure," I chuckled. "Maybe one day."

"I'll pay the rent until you can manage it with your donations. I'll call my realtor and see what we can find." I didn't believe her. Not that I thought she was lying, but WHO SAYS THAT?

She didn't mention it again that weekend, but guess who called me Monday morning? There IS enough—and with that call, we began searching for a Manhattan space for our pajamas, books, and visiting children.

Friends, family, and volunteers helped us turn a large one-room studio on East 39th Street in Manhattan's Murray Hill neighborhood into an enchanting, mesmerizing Reading Center! Here was a place where the children in New York City could come and be read to and then take new pajamas and books back to where they'd sleep that night. What made our new Reading Center especially wonderful was a giant mural of beloved characters including Cinderella, Ariel from *The Little Mermaid*, and Minnie and Mickey Mouse that had the children swoon, giggle, and cheer as they walked in the door. It was painted with love by the artists of pajama manufacturer and Pajama Program supporter Richard Leeds International.

Our beloved Yonkers volunteers carried on at their small site while we expanded our "office" in the larger Manhattan space. Claudia paid our rent for three years until we had an ample nest egg to carry on all by ourselves.

Demo and I were still making visits to the park bench to dream

88888888

8888888888888888888

and plan, and with Demo's encouragement, I was now visualizing a date with Oprah Winfrey in the flesh. I laughed at his suggestion, but he was intent on my taking this seriously.

"See it happening, feel what it's like to sit next to Oprah," he urged. "You have a good story, and you've said over and over it would be a dream come true. All of you are working so hard, there's no reason to laugh at the concept that you could be on her show to tell more people about these children and what you're doing."

Getting on Oprah's show was a long shot, to say the least. The magazine was one thing, but on the celebrated Oprah couch? I chuckled. What are the chances I'd be on her show? But after he made me stop laughing, I focused.

———

ALMOST DAILY, I imagined being a guest on *The Oprah Winfrey Show*, mostly just to appease Demo. I closed my eyes and pictured sitting in front of her on the stage, answering her questions, telling her about the little girl who started it all, and talking about Oprah's favorite topic: finding your purpose. I got *into* it. I *felt* what it would *feel* like to sit next to her, I *heard* her voice clearly, I answered her questions, and she listened to me intently. I looked at her eyes, and I saw *into* them, caring and sensitive. I felt deeply connected to her, calmed by her love and empathy. We were heart-to-heart in my visions, and it felt more and more real every time. We were having effortless conversations in my mind, and I wasn't a bit nervous. Now, that's a dream!

I'd heard about vision boards but never tried making one. Then I read *The Secret* and was intrigued by a story about a man who made a vision board, and after looking at it every day, his dream came true. It sounded too simple to be true, but I had nothing to lose and a lot to gain.

I bought dozens of magazines and spread them out all over the living room floor, along with markers and scissors and poster board. A vision board is so simple yet literally has the power of the universe behind it. If you believe thoughts are things, and that what you desire in your heart of hearts can come to fruition if you focus your intention on it, then a vision board is for you. A large poster board, photos and pictures of the life you want, and a marker are all you need. But, and this is a big BUT, you absolutely need to *feel* a pull in your heart toward each and every photo and picture you cut out and put on that magic board. It is believed that the energy between your heart and the universe will bring that visual to life. I began scouring the magazines to make my board. And I knew I had to *feel* each and every image.

My first vision board was a hodge-podge of things I liked and wanted both for Pajama Program and personally. I took my 20" x 30" foam board and started with a photo of me and Demo right in the center. Next to it, I put one of my favorite photos of a child to whom I read, a smiling little girl in pigtails squeezing her new pajamas to her chest.

I then pasted pictures of everything I dreamed of: a beautiful home on the beach with a giant outdoor pool to do my laps every morning; exotic places I wanted to visit, including islands in the Caribbean, Sicily, Greece, Prague, Sedona, and Santa Barbara; my family at our happiest times; Demo and I laughing as we walked along the beach on our trip to Costa Rica; girlfriends sharing dinner and wine. I cut out words like LOVE, LAUGH, ADVENTURE, SUCCESS, JOY, LIGHT, TRANQUILITY, and FREEDOM and strategically taped them around my images. Finally, I got up my courage to put a big picture of Oprah Winfrey from *O* magazine on the board.

At first, I'd been tentative about making a vision board. I felt like I was fooling myself into thinking this could work, that I was only doing it to assure myself that my life could be normal again without the constant money worries and uncertain future job prospects. But as I sat on our living room floor with dozens of cut-up magazines, scissors, tape, and glue sticks, I really got into it. A thrill ran up my spine as I really took in all the images I'd chosen. All of a sudden, I knew for sure that things were going to happen!

The board went up on my bureau so every morning as I dressed, it stared me right in the face. It took a little while to get comfortable looking at it and *believing* in it, but as the weeks passed, I let myself feel what the pictures touched in me, and I started to believe.

All the photos I put on my board represented things I loved, but more importantly each picture I looked at seemed real to me, like it somehow was already a part of me, a part of my life. I felt excited and empowered, like everything was possible. When I looked at the board, I was better able to fight off the worry and stress of what we were growing and all the unknowns still ahead. I knew that board had life.

The Heart of the Matter

* Make your vision board. Now.

WHEN YOU'RE GOING through a transformation or you want things to change in either your career or your personal life, you have to see it in your mind and feel it in your heart first. Display what you see and feel as a collage of pictures and keep it in front of you. It will help you organize your thoughts. Believe those pictures are your life now, and they will become your life. Sound crazy? Yup. Does it work? Yup.

* Embrace what comes out of left field.

DON'T BE SURPRISED by shocking gifts from out of nowhere! Making the commitment to transform your life into a more fulfilling one doesn't mean everything will fall into place with ease. Unfortunately, fear, uncertainty, and anxiety take hold of your body from time to time. However, you'll find that when your actions are "on purpose," incredible surprises fall into your lap to appease the doubt.

Chapter 12

The *O* Factor

O ne day in the spring of 2007, I was working alone at my desk in our New York City Reading Center. The phone rang, and I picked it up: "This is Genevieve at Pajama Program. Can I help you?"

"Hi, I'm Alyssa from *The Oprah Winfrey Show*. Do you have a minute?" asked the woman on the other end.

I don't know how I didn't drop the phone and pass out. Most days, the Reading Center is chock-full of people buzzing around. This day, there was no one there with me, not one single person to whom I could silently scream, or mouth, or wave wildly: "OH MY GOD, THIS IS THE *OPRAH* SHOW!!!"

"Sure," I answered as calmly as I could. My chest was going to explode if I didn't exhale.

"We've been hearing a lot about Pajama Program, and I know you were in our magazine awhile back. I'd love to ask you a few questions."

"Sure," I said again.

I marvel now at how I made any sense at all in that conversation, telling my story bit by bit. It was a miracle that I was even able to speak and breathe at the same time. Nothing short of divine intervention, I tell you.

We spoke for quite a while, and it turned out OK, I guess, because at the end, Alyssa said she would be calling me again. She told me people had been writing to the show about this woman (me!!) who was giving pajamas and books to children who didn't have any. I was touched and shocked that people cared that much and were willing to plead my case to complete strangers.

I got off the phone and swore myself to secrecy. I am a firm believer in the power of jinxing something away, and there was no way I was going to jinx it. Keeping silent was the hardest thing I'd ever done, but I did it.

Alyssa called back several times over the next three weeks, and I felt myself inching closer and closer to Oprah's couch with each call. Finally, she said, "Before I book you for the show I have to ask you if there's anything you need to tell me. If there is, you need to tell me right now."

I knew why she asked me that. It was right after an author endorsed by Oprah and interviewed on her show was accused of fabricating parts of his memoir. Oprah wasn't going to take a chance on someone else who might be a fraud.

"Nope!" I said, and I felt like I was just about to win the lottery.

She discussed show dates and travel arrangements. Then I held my breath.

"Can I tell my husband?" I whispered.

"Yes," she laughed. "Of course you can!"

I got the Oprah "you're booked" call in front of the Morgan

Library & Museum on Madison Avenue. Every time I pass it, I still feel like I can fly.

I told Demo, my parents and siblings, my coworker Terri, and Sharon from Pajama Program's board, along with just a few close friends. Demo was over the moon, and together we laughed and cried the entire week before we got on the plane to Chicago for the show's taping. I asked my mom to come with us. She's a huge Oprah fan, and my inspiration for Pajama Program, so I knew this would be the trip of a lifetime for her. Terri was so excited, she just kept repeating, "This is your dream . . . this is your dream!"

Demo and my mom made the trip with me on a very cold April evening. Our flight was delayed due to bad weather, and we all grew increasingly worried since our taping was early the next morning. What if the flight is canceled? What if we crash? What if, what if . . . ? But we got on the plane, found our seats, and got settled in.

I'd made it clear to Demo and my mom that we were not to tell anyone on the flight why we were going to Chicago—no jinxing allowed. We could chat with people, just no Oprah chatting! Terri, who was also coming to the show, took a separate flight because her daughter and family were in town visiting from Wisconsin. I didn't know it then, but Terri knew about what Oprah had planned for us.

Terri had been receiving phone calls from people around the country who were on a mission to "collect as many pajamas as they could without Genevieve finding out." Our desks sat face-to-face as she answered those calls, careful not to let on to me. She didn't know the whole picture, but she knew it was "Oprah-related."

We landed about midnight, starving, and found a Chinese restaurant near our hotel that was still open. Alyssa had been keeping track of our flight progress and told me to call her no matter what time we landed. I called.

"Welcome to Chicago!" she said. "I'll give you a quick rundown of what to expect tomorrow."

After that, the only thing I remember from the entire conversation was "...and then Oprah will call you to come up from the audience, and you'll hop onto the stool on stage."

Now I was terrified. All I could think about was finding a way to gently hop onto a stool next to Oprah Winfrey in front of millions of people. I didn't visualize it that way; it was supposed to be a couch. I didn't sleep all night.

———

THE FIRST THING the limo driver said in the morning was "*Oprah* show, right?" We said yes. He said, "I knew it because you have all your teeth, and some of the people I drive to other shows here don't!" We laughed so hard that we broke through our nervousness.

We slowly pulled up to Harpo Studios, and my heart started to race. We were there. It was really happening. Unless the world blew up, I'd be on *The Oprah Winfrey Show* telling Oprah and the world about the children of Pajama Program. We were escorted through the huge corridors by a young lady who was lovely but seemed nervous and confused. Taking direction from someone on her headset, she kept changing our course, from one hallway to another. I remember thinking that she must be new because she didn't seem to know her way around.

We finally arrived at the green room via a strangely circuitous route. Producers, makeup artists, and legal reps all arrived at our heels. My hair and makeup were done flawlessly, we signed nondisclosure notices, and we listened to the rundown of how the show would go. I would be the first guest of three and was briefed on what questions Oprah would ask me. I was told again that Oprah would start the show with me and would call me up from my seat to hop onto the stool next to her. Those words "hop onto the stool" made me sweat again.

Demo and I were separated from my mom and Terri, who were taken to their seats in the audience. We were escorted to two chairs right outside the audience door, where we were told to wait until the rest of the audience members were seated before us. I focused on staying calm. I closed my eyes, repeating soothing words to myself to keep from fainting.

"Peace, peace, stay centered, breathe . . . in . . . out . . . ," I said. I turned to Demo, and he was crying! I panicked.

"Stop crying," I demanded. "You're supposed to keep me calm and you're crying??! We're going in there any minute!"

"I'm so happy for you," he said. "This is what we hoped would happen one day, and I am so proud of you! Don't you remember how we sat in the park and talked about the possibility of getting on *Oprah*? Now it's happening!"

I thought back to our times on the bench, when we dreamed about how a segment on Oprah's show could change everything. We were doing all we could to keep Pajama Program going, but each day we hoped for that boost, that jolt to keep us alive and strong. And now here we were.

The signal came, and a young female usher with a headset started to escort us to our seats. As we walked through the audience, the show's announcer introduced me and Demo over the loudspeaker, which made me self-conscious. Shockingly, I walked without tripping over my feet, my mind still split in two: one side directing my body to walk calmly to the seat the usher pointed me to in the front row, and the other side screaming in my head, "You're on *OPRAH!* You're on *OPRAH!!!*"

The audience was clapping, but I thought nothing of it; I assumed it was just because they had a CLAP sign. Sure, it was really nice of them to do this, but little did I know what was going to happen.

The producers were ready to start the show. Oprah was introduced and came out in her flat shoes carrying her high heels, making everyone laugh.

The show started. Oprah displayed beautiful posters of Pajama Program children, images from the children who were part of Hour Children. She gave me a brief introduction and called me up to the stage. It was the moment I'd ruminated over endlessly, the thing I was most nervous about, but I hopped onto the stool like a pro. I didn't fall or stumble or embarrass myself in any way. I knew then that it would be okay. The hard part was over.

I remember looking at Oprah and feeling relaxed, like she and I were real friends. She told me she liked my jacket, that green was her favorite color. I told her my friend Nova Lorraine made it for me for the show. Oprah was so easy to talk to, so radiant and funny! I couldn't believe this woman who changes lives, this iconic, maternal figure who gives voice to so many, was really listening to me. She asked me to share my purpose with her and invited me not only into her life but also into the lives of all those who trusted her.

I was humbled, and so grateful.

Oprah's eyes were huge, and they took me right into her soul as I answered her questions. You know how people always say be in the moment? I really and truly was while I was sitting with her. Oprah's aura is full of love, and her presence seems to cause time to stand still. I actually thought to myself, "Wow, what big eyes she has.

I'm being drawn to them like a magnet." It was so strange because I know my mouth was moving and I was able to speak to Oprah in coherent sentences on the show, but at the same time the other half of my brain was thinking, "You're talking to Oprah Winfrey!" As she listened to my little story, I thought about her eyes being so huge that I could see and feel tremendous compassion and power coming through them!

Oprah got it, she understood what I was doing and why. She affirmed that my purpose was legitimate. She gave me such an incredible gift, the realization that no one's story is trivial, including mine. And even small gestures, whether kind or cruel, can change someone's life.

I felt safe in Oprah's space and I felt empowered to live my life on purpose. I wanted to sit next to her for the rest of the day and savor her light. I knew I could do what I had to do now for the children, and I also knew they'd have to pry me off that stool when it was time for me to leave.

In the middle of the interview, which was going according to the plan I was given, Oprah suddenly announced to me, "What you don't know is . . . about seven days ago we, meaning our producers, called up this studio audience and told them about your tremendous acts, what you've done of love, so we challenged this audience to pay it forward by bringing as many new pajamas as they could to the studio today."

She went on, "This is the catch: They were only allowed, this audience, to buy one pair . . . and then they had to be resourceful and see if they could find other people who wanted to donate more than that. So, my producers this morning, they wouldn't tell me how many PJs everybody brought, but everybody seems pretty happy this morning. So, Dean, the envelope. I'm going to tell you how many pajamas."

The audience went wild—they were all in on the big surprise.

Celebratory music started playing, and someone handed Oprah a large, sealed gold envelope that she opened slowly and dramatically, and with a shocked look on her face revealed the number: 32,046!

I was stunned. So was Oprah. Her eyes rolled back as she repeated, "How great! How great!" I screamed and covered my face with my hands and started to cry. Everyone was standing and cheering and clapping wildly.

Enormous bins, decorated jumbo containers, and racks and racks of clothing were rolled out, overflowing with children's pajamas that had been arriving for the past five days. Oprah quieted everyone and then asked a few people how they did it. Some collected thousands through email chains, others called retailers and manufacturers who donated pajamas, and some collected pajamas from friends and family, who brought hundreds to their homes.

The excitement in the studio was incredible. Every single person there, and everyone they contacted, cared for the children. They wanted them to feel cozy and safe at bedtime; they knew the children deserved to be remembered. Between the loads of packages and letters from *Parenting* magazine readers, and now these thousands of donations from Oprah lovers, I was astounded by how much love strangers felt for these children. And I was the lucky one who was going to be able to convey that love to thousands of children who were desperate for it.

Oprah told us there were pajamas everywhere in the Harpo building, in every room and in every hallway—and that's why the sweet young lady whom I thought didn't know the way to the green room was taking so many sudden turns. They were hiding them from me!

Before we left Harpo Studios, the producers asked Terri and me where they should send all the pajamas. Terri and I were silent and, surprisingly, still standing upright after that question. Neither of us had given a thought to what would happen next. I was sure my voice was quivering when I responded, "Can we email you the address when we get back to New York?" Terri, Demo, and I were stymied. What address indeed??!!

The entire plane ride home, Terri and I searched our brains agonizing over who could hold more than 32,000 pajamas. Exactly how many boxes was that??!! We came up with nil. We deplaned, now fraught with anxiety, to find a message from the *Oprah* producer.

"Don't worry about one address for the boxes," the producer said. "Instead, why don't you send us a list of all the places you'd like the pajamas to go, and we will divide them up and send them to your list." The magic of Oprah.

The Heart of the Matter

- Cherish once-in-a lifetime experiences.

SOMETIMES THE PLANETS align PERFECTLY! We have all had unbelievable experiences that feel out of body, but the truth is, they *aren't* unbelievable, and we are indeed still in our bodies! I've learned so many lessons about purpose, passion, meaning, belief, faith, and the human connection, and while each is powerful in its own right, together they are an enormous force when we live on purpose. Trust yourself, and the universe and the joy of manifesting what's on your vision board will be truly "believable."

- The human connection strikes again.

MORE THAN 32,000 pairs of pajamas made their way to Oprah's stage because several hundred audience members, led by one powerhouse of a woman, were asked to help. The power of one? You know it now—it's the power of one another!

Chapter 13

The Slot Machine

wo weeks later, on the day our *Oprah* segment aired, my family and friends gathered around the television at my sister's home in New Rochelle. No one could sit still as we watched the clock tick down to showtime. Millions of fans—including my family and friends—would soon see what happened in Chicago.

I had been sworn to secrecy until after the program aired, but our local paper ran a story that morning about a "surprise for local resident Genevieve Piturro on *Oprah* today at 4 o'clock!"

My sister's living room fell silent as the *Oprah* graphics rolled across the TV screen. There was squealing and giggling as *Oprah* introduced my story and our interview began. As everything was slowly revealed, screams and hollers (mirroring the audience's) filled the room until I thought the roof would blow off! Everyone's laughter turned into tears.

Apparently, everyone watching *Oprah* felt the same way because

donations and emails flowed in at record speed and didn't stop
for days.

In Brooklyn, Terri watched the show with her family gathered for Passover. After watching "a slot machine jackpot reaction"
among viewers, she turned to one of the young caterers she'd hired
to help at home that day and said, "Do you need another part-time
job? I think we'll need some help!"

Kathleen started working for us the next day, and shortly after, we
hired her friend Candice. In addition, hundreds of volunteers, chapter
presidents, and others who started after Oprah aired are still with us.

The show was a hit, and they aired it again nine months later
in December. We were floored by the responses we received in
cash donations, pajama drives across the country, and from interested individuals who helped us establish new chapters in Nevada,
Maine, Idaho, Kansas, Texas, Arizona, Florida, Colorado, Tennessee,
Pennsylvania, and California.

Oprah really does change everything (thank you, Oprah!), and
her viewers' heartfelt letters propelled us to new heights.

> "I watched the *Oprah* show and was amazed at the
> work you are doing with the Pajama Program . . .
> I would be extremely interested in helping you set
> up a chapter in WV . . . I told my husband, I told all
> my friends, I quite frankly told everyone that would
> listen and that was just since yesterday."
>
> —Megan, West Virginia

> "My husband and I watched the *Oprah* show
> together . . . I immediately related to Gen in that
> I am career driven, married in my 30s, and never

had the desire to have children of my own . . . When I found out that Maine did not have a chapter I started thinking about starting one . . . So far we are providing pajamas to two domestic violence shelters, one homeless shelter, and one children's home that serves more than 1,425 children throughout central Maine. I can't tell you how much helping children fills me up every day."

—Karen, Maine chapter president

"I first learned of the Pajama Program in 2007 from the *Oprah* show and . . . couldn't get its mission out of my mind. Having two small children who look forward all day to getting into their PJs and reading books at bedtime, I just couldn't imagine that there were children somewhere in this world that didn't have the same loving comfort that my children had . . . I just knew I had to reach out to offer my help to the Pajama Program. Somehow, I get the feeling that the Pajama Program will bring me and my family more than I could ever possibly give back to it."

—Jill from Pennsylvania

"The impact Pajama Program and Genevieve Piturro had being featured on the *Oprah* show has been tremendous. From the moment the show was aired, we have received countless emails and calls from people all across Illinois offering both volunteer hours as well as new pajamas."

—Shirlee, Illinois chapter president

WE ALSO RECEIVED a very special thank-you from a shelter staffer in Plano, Texas, who received pajamas from *Oprah:*

> "Thank you so much for all the work you and your group do for the underserved children in this country. Your Pajama Program ensures our children at Angelheart Children's Shelter sleep in fresh, new pajamas. This is extremely important to our kids who have suffered abuse and neglect. Many of these kids arrive with only the clothing they wear, so a new pair of PJs symbolizes their 'fresh start' on their road to healing. Fresh Start is the name we have given our clothing program and your project is now a fundamental part of that work . . . You and your staff are our own special angels."

IT MOVED ME to hear from viewers of the *Oprah* show who were inspired to start their own nonprofits, some of whom also wanted to leave their jobs and find something that would give them a sense of purpose.

I discovered that more and more people were dissatisfied with their current lives. People would tell me that they, too, wondered if the path they were on was fulfilling enough for the rest of their lives. Like me, they asked, "Is this all there is to life?" I had been one of them just a few short years ago. Many wrote to ask me if I had any advice for them. Wow, advice?

I was barely making sense of what I was doing for myself, swaying between self-assured days and not-so-sure days. I was petrified to give advice. What if I got it wrong? What if I steered someone astray? Still, I wanted to help, to let them know they weren't alone. I remembered the rejection of my friend at dinner the first time I revealed my secret. I would *never* do that to someone.

My mentors had propped me up, and now it was my turn to be a supporter. I felt a camaraderie with these viewers and was compelled to urge them on. I answered phone calls and emails, and I'm still in contact with several of them to this day. I've watched them grapple with some of the same issues I faced at the start; as they grow, I grow, knowing we need one another to lean on. Here are excerpts from some of the emails I received:

> *"Hello my name is Kristina . . . I can relate to your story in many ways. I'm 36 and . . . know that [my current job] is not my true life's calling. My life is most purposeful when I am giving myself away in service to others . . . I'm currently in the 'creating the vision' phase; what does this look like for my life, and how can I make a living doing it. I would love to talk to you about your journey and gain some insight/guidance on what my next steps should be as I pursue this shift into philanthropy."*

> *"Hi Genevieve,*
>
> *Your Pajama Program . . . has inspired me to start my organization, SOCKS 4 TOTS. It all started back . . . [when] I saw you on* The Oprah Winfrey Show. *Watching you sparked my heart to finally go after my dream, the dream of helping homeless children . . . . At that very moment, God*

gave me the name SOCKS 4 TOTS . . . I finally received my
not-for-profit papers on July 26, 2007, what a blessing . . .
Thank you for your example of caring while living in such
an uncaring world . . . Love, Laverne, President & CEO,
SOCKS 4 TOTS Inc."

———

WHAT COULD BE better than being on *Oprah*? Nothing, I thought, and now more than ever, we needed to find a way to sustain these new heights. We started to receive inquiries from manufacturers and retailers, and our presentations had to be more formal, a lot more sophisticated, and a whole lot more comprehensive.

I had contacted the children's clothing company Carter's when I moved into the cubicle at David's firm because it was the go-to children's pajama brand. I felt in my heart that they would understand the urgent need for Pajama Program. My calls and letters went unanswered in those early days, but I understood it takes time for perfect matches to be made—after all, didn't I wait nearly 20 years to meet my soulmate?

A wonderful partnership with another company, Scholastic, was created in 2008 after I met Betsy Howie. (Neither of us can recall if I called her or she found us!) We clicked immediately and knew we wanted to work together. Betsy had Scholastic's Classrooms Care program engage all their schools as hosts for pajama drives. Since then, thousands of schools from across the country have rallied together to donate more than 260,000 pairs of new pajamas.

Each year, Scholastic Reading Club has committed to matching those pajama donations with books, and even exceeded those donations, with more than 500,000 provided to our program.

We were also thrilled to receive a call in 2008 from a woman at the TV network Sprout. Having no children of my own, I had no idea what Sprout was, but I quickly learned! The 24-hour preschool television network became Pajama Program's national media partner for several years for The Great Sprout Tuck-In, a prosocial initiative that extended Sprout's "good night" mission and encouraged families to share in the spirit of giving through public service announcements, nighttime programming, and a donation-match program to benefit Pajama Program.

Life dramatically changed after I put "OPRAH" nice and big on my vision board. Now I felt a sort of electricity, a buzzing in the air every day. I could actually feel the fragments of what I still needed for Pajama Program swirling around me, including corporate partners, additional staff and chapter presidents, and funding for more groups of children to visit our Reading Center, waiting like puzzle pieces to find each other and interlock.

I knew athletes used visualization techniques and that celebrity coach and author Tony Robbins touted it as a significant part of his training with highly successful people. I used to think, "I'm not an athlete or a highly successful individual, so what's visualization going to do for me?" In my mind, visualization was for people who had achieved a higher level of success.

But the moment I glued Oprah's picture to my vision board, I started to believe bigger and better gifts would come to help me achieve my goals if I could see them in my mind and also in front of me every day. Like a lucky charm, in August 2008, our *Oprah* segment aired for the third time.

We were determined to move Pajama Program into the realm of established nonprofits. We needed to get ourselves into a stable position, a place where we could breathe a little easier, where I could sleep two or three hours a night without waking up in a cold sweat worrying whether we had enough money.

That's precisely when a thoughtful and compassionate young woman named Tanya called from Carter's! A young mom herself, she called to say she'd heard about Pajama Program, had seen the Oprah segment, and wanted to throw around a few ideas! Carter's started donating thousands of pajamas, and soon I was invited to meet Mike Casey, Carter's chairman and CEO. That meeting marked one of my all-time favorite days, ever.

After hearing my story, Mr. Casey looked at me and said, "It's simple. All I want is for every child to go to bed in warm, clean pajamas. Let's do this."

It was the start of a beautiful and symbiotic relationship, not only between Pajama Program and Carter's but between our children and Carter's staff, and the millions of happy Carter's consumers who knew all too well that no child should have to go to sleep in soiled, ragged clothes.

Over our 10-year partnership, Carter's and their shoppers have donated millions of pajamas to our children and raised funds to help us grow.

The Heart of the Matter

- The secret of the power of one.

WE'VE ALL HEARD people talk about how the power of one person can change things. I have found that while it does takes one idea and maybe one person to start something big, it takes a whole lot more people to start a movement and make a difference in thousands of lives. There is power in each of us, yes, but as you've read in these pages, when we invite the human connection in, a tremendous force is ignited. The power of one begins the journey, and the power of one another takes it home.

- Top that!

IT MAY BE difficult to top the highs you'll experience from encounters with amazing individuals who have the ability to support you and multiply your reach tenfold, but you can harness that exhilaration to reach even further and change even more. Express your gratitude earnestly, and use your newfound confidence to make a plan!

- The mentee becomes the mentor.

LEADERSHIP IS MEASURED not by how much you advance, but by how much you advance others. No doubt you've been the recipient of advice and guidance from someone who walked your path before you. There will come a time for you to pass along that advice, and more of your own to another person who comes calling. Give freely, there's no competition to be worried about here. There's enough to go around.

Chapter 14

The Ones Who
Know the Score

After flying into the stratosphere with Oprah, then partnering with Scholastic and Carter's, there came a point where I needed to examine the different age groups Pajama Program served and carefully develop a thoughtful strategy to serve each one.

While I could never walk even a few steps away from the children Pajama Program serves, I realized that we were focusing almost exclusively on the little ones. When we opened our first Reading Center in Yonkers, we dove into planning programs for the younger children who needed help learning to read. This seemed pretty easy—books plus pajamas plus little kids plus a snack. All we had to do was lie on the floor and read their new books with them, and they were happy. They felt special, and they were learning words and reading in a comforting "party" atmosphere. So many little faces were full of sadness, eyes deadened, and wishes denied. Books could open their imaginations, and that's where hope might be able to enter one more time. With every page we turned together, we, too, had hope—hope that they would sleep in peace and wake up with a lighter heart.

I saw clearly now that we had overlooked a group of profoundly at-risk older children, who faced different challenges and had different needs: teens in foster care. These children—and they were still children—always held a very special place in my heart, and for a long time, I had an extremely difficult time finding ways to help heal them.

———

THE PRE-TEENS AND teenagers we meet in the program are visibly uncomfortable in their own skin, something so many of us remember from our own adolescence. The youngest children tug at our hearts. They're full of hope—so happy to be paid attention to, so excited to get a gift. But as they get older, their hope often dwindles, and they are no longer innocent little children so sure that tomorrow will be better. Too many times they become lost.

Many tweens and teens in the system have been abused physically or emotionally or both. Some of them have had to endure the heartbreak of a father leaving, never to be heard from again, or a drug-addicted mother who spends days and nights high, out cold on a couch. Or, they face one of the worse scenarios imaginable: a parent's suicide.

It's a sad fact that as children in foster care age, it becomes less likely that people will take them into their home or adopt them, if that is possible. Many people don't want to expose their families to children who have experienced trauma and the issues they face. Sometimes in order for one child to be adopted, there's a sibling that's part of the package. I've seen children of all ages for whom that's true, and a lot of families aren't prepared for it or interested.

I remember one year around Christmas when we gave pajamas and books to children in a group home, and a television station wanted to cover it. It's rare for a group home to agree to media coverage because their children, as minors, are generally off-limits. In this one case, the group home made a request. They would allow two preteen brothers to appear and talk about what it meant to receive our gifts if the home was given the chance to let viewers know these boys were available for adoption. I thought this was a chance for these boys to meet a family who would be overjoyed to provide them with a home full of love and let them start a new life. But no, the home received only toys from kind viewers who wanted to make sure the children at least had a nice Christmas.

As the months went by, our Yonkers Reading Center volunteers settled into their assigned groups with children after school and on weekend mornings. Meanwhile, I began to walk around the ANDRUS property and ask questions. There were five cottages, each housing 10 to 12 children, but only one of the five cottages was for teen girls. I didn't know how the gender ratio compared to other group homes or foster care in general, but I remember thinking that those girls must feel very isolated.

I decided to ask the administration if we could form a reading program for these girls, and the response was a resounding YES! Their answer was my first clue that these girls were definitely feeling alone and maybe even a little lost.

Then it hit me. When I was 13, I also felt lost, even though I had a loving family, a secure home, and friends and teachers who cared. When I thought about how insecure, unattractive, fat, lonely, and nerdy I felt at their age, I was ashamed of myself that I'd neglected these girls and added to their loneliness. Here we were having fun a few doors away with all the little kids, making these girls feel left out in yet another way.

We set up our first after-school reading party with a group of 11 girls. I was eager to make them feel like they belonged, that they were just like other kids in 7th and 8th grade, even though these children attended school on the grounds of their group home. This was my chance to wrap them all in my arms like I did the little ones and let them know I cared. I could never believe I could make it all right for any of these kids.

Sadly, it was incredibly difficult to get them to even sit near me, let alone embrace the idea of me in their lives at all. For days, they wouldn't read or even talk when I was there. One look at the scowls on their faces when the staff forced them into the room made me feel inept and utterly preposterous. I tried to insist that this could be fun, but I felt like such an oblivious phony.

Needless to say, after 10 minutes of cajoling and trying to convince the girls to "read just a little out loud," I stopped.

"What would you like to talk about?" I asked them, hoping and praying at least one girl would answer me as I sat there, a complete stranger. We remained in silence for a long time until one of the staff saved me and said, "Tell Miss Genie about the songs you write."

I perked up. "Songs? You write songs?"

"We write rap," one of the older girls corrected the staff member.

"Rap is great!" I said, adding, "Tell me one."

I could hear every word as one shy girl sitting in a lumpy armchair quietly spoke hers out loud. There was something about a father who left without a word and a boyfriend who cheated. Another girl sitting on an ottoman in the middle of the room jumped in, stealing the attention, and rapped long and angrily about a mom who was drunk. One girl's rap led to another, each girl trying to convince us hers was better, all of them forlorn.

They each wanted to share—these raps were their badges of courage and a way for them to express themselves. The quiet group soon became rowdy, too rowdy. One girl insulted another girl's lyrics as immature, and the offended girl lunged at her until one of the staff separated them and ended our session. A few of the girls were clearly sorry the evening was cut short, and I felt bad leaving early.

"But this is good," I remember thinking to myself as I walked back to my car. These girls want to speak up. There's something here I can do to help them. I just have to find a way.

And just like when I was 13, I thought to myself, "I hope they like me."

The night before I next went to meet the girls, I tossed and turned, unable to sleep. I feared another embarrassing and lame afternoon with girls who rolled their eyes at me. I decided to use a different approach.

"Who knows what rap is?" I asked the group, which had now dwindled to eight girls who remained interested, or at least curious. No answer.

"Rap is poetry," I declared. Still no response. I feigned camaraderie and continued, "So, here's what we're going to do over the next five weeks—we're going to read poetry and write rap."

I handed out books by great female poets like Emily Dickinson, Maya Angelou, Dorothy Parker, Alice Walker, and Emily Brontë. Still, the girls were reluctant and moaned in their boredom. They felt absolutely no connection between their raps and the poems of these women until they started reading a little and realized that the one thing all these poets wrote about was what they wrote about, too: LOVE. Finding love, losing love, needing love. And the worst: unrequited love.

Love, and being loved, was what these girls thought about. Deep down, they somehow still believed that even though they had been rejected, scorned, and betrayed, an unconditional love for them existed somewhere. And they were determined to find it.

The girls found a connection with these poets and weren't shy about voicing their opinions about which writer was scorned worse, loved less, gave too much, or was a total sucker for love. They told me they could write better poems and that they could rap and sing them, too. When I told them I had brand-new pajamas for them that night, I saw a few smiles sneak onto their faces.

That day, our Poetry Plus Program was created. It encouraged teenage girls who had been removed from a family environment to talk about their feelings while at the same time raising their self-esteem.

That first group of girls was a huge challenge for me. I often found myself thinking that I was not the right person to run the program. They looked at me like I was an alien, like I had no business trying to figure them out, save them, or be their friend. Maybe they were right. What did I know about any of them or their lives? It wasn't easy getting them to read the famous poets, but it did get easier to persuade them to write more poetry themselves—though we called it "rap" and "songs."

I learned from my experience with teens in group homes that the kids who had seniority ruled. Newbies were either painfully shy, withdrawn, or extremely rambunctious, demanding to be heard from day one. I never knew what kind of environment I was walking into. Would the girls be getting along well and looking forward to our session, or was there a major upset with one or two of them who were being punished, leaving the remaining girls depressed and lackluster? The odds were 50/50.

No, it wasn't easy, but there were encouraging moments. I noticed some of the girls doodling, and when I asked them if I could see the doodles, I discovered some amazing art and talent. A friend of mine published a monthly teen magazine written and illustrated by and for teens, and I knew she could help. She met the girls and proposed a fantastic project.

Some of the girls would write poems and others would illustrate them, and then she would publish it as a magazine complete with cover art and a title of their choosing! Some of the girls immediately loved the idea and started vying for their poem/rap/song to be on the first page, while others withdrew and refused to have their work on display.

No one was forced into the project, but guess what? Over the next four weeks, as the most outspoken and bold girls aggressively pushed for their poems or artwork to have center stage in the magazine, every single girl—even the least assertive—fought to be included in it! It had become a lesson for each of them in how to find their own way to be included and accepted. The girls became more supportive of each other, and while there was still competition, it wasn't as degrading or nasty as in the early days of their sessions together. We had a way to go before we could say they worked as a team, but thanks to the girls' caring and patient caregivers and therapists, there was definitely more laughing with each other rather than at each other as our project progressed.

———

OUR TEEN PROGRAMS were designed to reinforce feelings of well-being and self-confidence. Poetry Plus was our first such program, and we invited special guests, including self-esteem coaches, writers, publishers, and men and women with careers of interest to the girls and boys, like dancers and chefs, to participate. Our goal was to encourage the belief that with enough support and encouragement, they can move mountains. And boy, do teens love their pajamas! One donor, the Paganelli family, who welcomed a teen boy from a group home into their family, made getting teens pajamas their way of giving back. Every December for a decade, they asked each of their 300+ holiday guests to bring a pair of pajamas for the teens of Pajama Program! They encouraged our teens by sharing so much of their love with them in this special way.

The girls in the Poetry Plus Program wrote movingly about missing lost loved ones, about loneliness, about regret, pride, and being grateful. In their poems, they always seemed to ask, "Will my heart heal?"

In order for them to start healing, they needed to start opening up and sharing their deepest, darkest fears. As soon as they did, they realized they had company in their feelings, and in that company was solidarity.

I think that's the whole secret for all of us. We are so afraid we harbor feelings that no one else will understand, feelings that further alienate us from love, that we don't dare speak out loud. If only all of us knew at age 13 that the way to security and acceptance is to communicate our worst fears. By being vulnerable, we discover that we're not alone at all.

In our Poetry Plus Program, I saw girls and young ladies exhibit four basic traits: hope, courage, honesty, and vulnerability. These girls taught me time and time again what it takes to make change happen—inside ourselves and in the world. They are *hopeful* enough to wish for change. They find the *courage* to take a chance to look for it. And they are *honest* enough to wear their hearts on their sleeves, all while allowing us to see their *vulnerable* side as they look for what we all want: LOVE. These girls inspire me to be better.

One girl who deeply stirred me was Rachel, whom I met several years ago when she started coming to our Yonkers Reading Center. Rachel was then a 15-year-old aging out of the group home where she lived. She was told they were transferring her to another out-of-state group home, where the girls were as old as 18. She knew she didn't have a choice because they couldn't find any family members to take her in.

Rachel, who was very quiet and had few friends, tried to put on a brave front. She was desperately trying to be strong, and my heart broke for her every time I saw her.

She loved to practice her calligraphy alone in an armchair in a corner of the common area. One afternoon after our reading session, she shyly made her way over to me, and I could tell she was debating whether or not to ask me something. I was very curious and concerned, as she was more hesitant than usual. I also felt bad that she was having a hard time approaching me; I thought I'd failed her somehow. It took her a little while, but she eventually summoned up her courage.

"Miss Genie, will you show me how to apply makeup?" she quietly asked me. "The girls where they're sending me will be older than I am, and I want to fit in."

My first emotion was fury—how dare a mother leave her daughter to depend on strangers to love her, nurture her, teach her how to be a young lady, and now, show her how to put on makeup? I know there are hundreds of reasons why mothers leave their children, and as a society, we need to be understanding and compassionate toward these women. Yet in my mind—in that moment—there was no justifiable reason for Rachel's mother leaving her. Despite my anger, I tried to make peace with my feelings so I could be there for Rachel.

I knew Rachel's fears about her unknown future home—and roommates—were justified. She knew there was a good chance she wouldn't be immediately welcomed, and she was preparing for the worst.

I told Rachel to meet me the next afternoon when our Reading Center closed so my friend Netti—an expert makeup artist—and I could teach her all the tricks! The next afternoon, Netti and I turned our Reading Center into a salon, where we tried different hair and makeup techniques with Rachel. We did everything we could to boost Rachel's self-esteem, sharing stories of how Netti and I experimented with different looks for ourselves at her age, most of which were atrocious. I told Rachel I thought the epitome of a beautiful hairstyle was Farrah Fawcett hair—lots of long, glamorous layers trickling down my back—and that's exactly what I asked a stylist for when I was 15. I didn't wash or brush it for a week after I left that salon—I can only imagine how stringy it looked! Rachel cracked a smile, and it melted my heart.

In our "salon" that afternoon, it was my job to hold up a wall mirror while Netti showed Rachel how to fine-tune her eye makeup. I spent most of that time behind the mirror with tears running down my cheeks, thinking about Rachel's loneliness as she prepared to move.

We worked until we found the colors and methods that fit Rachel's personal style, and she practiced with tools of the trade until she felt confident that she could go it alone. Netti gave her a big cosmetic bag with goodies to keep practicing.

Rachel's hope, courage, honesty, and vulnerability empower me to keep walking beside these children, invisibly holding their hands as they grow from toddlers to teens.

Our teen programs are expanding in new ways, and this essay written by a 16-year-old at the culmination of one of our Poetry Plus Programs is my proof that if we listen and share, we are helping teens find themselves:

What Does it Take to Be Happy and Beautiful as a Woman Today

We have had many challenges, hurdles and experiences which have taught us that all women feel the same ways about being accepted, successful and worthy human beings.

To carry ourselves as ladies, that takes being humble and true to our real natures and self. We need to respect ourselves and others and think about others and what someone else may need, without always being worried or preoccupied with our own needs. Having good and positive posture, with an open heart area and feeling proud. Achieving these goals, we realize, is not always easy but the old ways didn't work. We know that and are glad that each day, day by day, we can work hard to improve ourselves, learn from our mistakes and for some, get their GED and finally, a paying job.

In order to be independent, we need to show that being accountable means something to us and that we can be counted on to do "the right thing." Having or asking for responsibilities is important to our building our confidence and for being able to depend on ourselves. For too long we relied on others, got our feedback from what we were doing with and for other people. We are learning a brand-new set of skills and "muscle memory" to carry us to our next levels in our personal and professional lives.

In summary, we all want to remember to say our daily affirmations, be humble and true to ourselves and our beautiful natures and to be accountable with the responsibilities we have taken on or have asked to assume. Being beautiful and happy people and women carries a lot of emotion since it has been a long and often bumpy road to get to where we are today; but well worth the efforts.

The Heart of the Matter

- Find the fix.

FINDING A SOLUTION to a problem can be complicated if it's awkward to ask questions. Often we truly want to help but are afraid of so many variables: how we'll be received, if we'll be rejected, if we'll find ourselves in a one-way conversation or worse, if we'll say or do the wrong thing. In order to do any good at all, we have to start somewhere. Lead with meaning, and look for a starting place of common ground. Making an effort to find similarities where you thought only differences existed may push you out of your comfort zone, but it's a genuine attempt to understand what the other person needs.

* Communication is the next step to the all-important feat of establishing trust where true camaraderie can occur.

As OUR VOLUNTEERS and I discovered when we first offered a reading party to teenage girls, we found common ground only when we stepped into their activity, writing rap songs. Later, we shared our own insecurities through stories of feeling like outcasts at their age. We discovered all of us are afraid to do or say the wrong things in front of our peers, even as adults. The girls allowed us into their world, little by little, until we couldn't distinguish whether the laughter and tears were theirs—or ours.

Chapter 15

What Hope Looks Like

We've come a long way over the past 20 years. In 2011, the year of our 10th anniversary, we organized a campaign to help children outside of the US, including those in Japan affected by the tsunami.

By 2012, we had 50 chapter presidents on our roster and distributed a record two million pajamas and books. More than 1,500 children came through our Reading Centers the next year. When the beautiful space Claudia helped us secure became too small, we opened a new Reading Center twice the size across the street with another magnificent mural designed by artists from Richard Leeds International.

The synergy of "tenacity and the universe" struck again in 2013 when Terri went to the taping of a new television show called *The Chew*. She came back to our Reading Center bubbling over with excitement.

"They have this host named Carla Hall who's a chef . . . and she was talking about being the auctioneer for her friend's event," she said, "[and] she was repeating how she was playing auctioneer . . . and she was FANTASTIC. We need HER for our next benefit!!"

I caught Terri's enthusiasm and instantly replied, "I'll go buy a rose and write her a letter, and you bring it to the show's studio tomorrow!"

"OK!" Terri replied, overjoyed.

A month went by and no word from Carla. We got someone else to play auctioneer. Then Carla called me, saying, "I'm so sorry to call so late . . . I loved your note and the rose . . . Do you still need an auctioneer?"

I was thrilled to get her call and disappointed, too. I told her we had hired someone else, and I invited her to come to our benefit. She was new in town and didn't know many people yet, so she graciously accepted. From her seat at our benefit that evening, she eagerly put her hand up during the auction and offered a new auction item: She would cook for a group of 10 people! Our guests loved her spontaneity, her charisma, her excitement, everything about her! Terri looked at me: "We need her on our board." Carla agreed.

That same year, we launched our One Million Good Nights campaign with Carter's, Scholastic, Target, Bob's Discount Furniture, and thousands of caring, compassionate individuals and companies across America.

As Carla's celebrity grew, she continued to elevate our presence with her recurring role as our auctioneer. She also chose Pajama Program as her charity when she appeared on *Who Wants to Be a Millionaire?* And Carla was incredibly generous when she invited some of the girls in our teen program to her restaurant to show them what a chef's job looks like!

Oprah, too, performed her magic for us once again by featuring Pajama Program on her "Where Are They Now?" series. That same year we brought 6,000 children through our three Reading Centers. By the end of 2014, we hit our One Million Good Nights campaign goal, with a grand total of four million pajamas and books given to children.

There's no better way to celebrate 15 years than by ringing the NASDAQ bell right smack in the middle of Times Square! And that's what we did in May 2016. I stood with our board members and a program volunteer holding her toddler in her arms. As I got the signal to hit the button that rings the bell, I placed my hand on top of the toddler's hand and, together, we rang that bell! We felt like the city, even the world, was celebrating with us. What a high! And then we opened our fourth Reading Center, this one in Atlanta, in 2017.

We have honored and worked with some special public figures who have shared their personal stories and their time with Pajama Program and our children. They include Jack Black, R.L. Stine, Ellen Burstyn, Judy Collins, Elizabeth Vargas, Soledad O'Brien, Al Roker, Susan Lucci, Kathy Dwyer (former president of Revlon's US division), and the Broadway producers and cast of *Annie*.

Through many of our compassionate ambassadors, we have shared pajamas and books with children in desperate situations in Australia, Bolivia, Bosnia, Brazil, Bulgaria, Canada, China, Colombia, Costa Rica, Ecuador, Indonesia, Greece, Honduras, Iraq, Israel, Italy, Jamaica, Japan, Liberia, London, Mexico, New Zealand, Nova Scotia, the Philippines, Siberia, Trinidad, Uganda, and Ukraine.

Yes, there is enough to go around.

As I write this, I am proud to tell you that as of May 2020, we have delivered more than seven million Good Nights filled with magical gifts of pajamas and books to children nationwide. We have 63 chapters run by volunteers in every state. And yet every day, I know we have more to do—as you'll see if you visit us at https://pajamaprogram.org.

———

DEMO AND I sold my co-op back in 2003, and instead of purchasing a dream home, we decided to rent a larger apartment. Today, we're still renters. We're at peace with our decisions and embrace the life we've built. Am I still amassing material things as a goal? Not so much. Yes, I still love to shop, but now it's more likely the final clearance rack of major department stores and T.J. Maxx. There's definitely something to be said for the high of scoring a major discount!

More and more, I spend my downtime learning to focus on my spiritual health rather than my physical trappings. Meditation has proven to be an incredible asset, and over time I've learned how to ground myself more quickly, especially in the moments when I feel overwhelmed and off balance.

One thing I am still learning: You have to be willing to delve deep, no matter how painful, in order to truly understand yourself. You need to look at your flaws and your strengths. You need to figure out what motivates you, what buoys you, and what takes you down.

Throughout this process of self-exploration, make sure not to sell yourself short. Recognize your kindnesses and how you have tenderly impacted the lives of people you care about. Accept your failures, forgive your mistakes, and keep going. Ask yourself about your insecurities, and seek out the answers bravely and honestly.

I learned those lessons from many of our honorees, such as actress Rosie Perez. Rosie spent her younger years in an orphanage and, despite some harrowing experiences, she never stopped believing she'd find a way out and up. I knew that she understood us when I read one particular passage in her 2015 memoir *Handbook for an Unpredictable Life: How I Survived Sister Renata and My Crazy Mother, and Still Came Out Smiling (with Great Hair)*.[2]

"Everyone quickly jumped into bed. No one tucked us in. No one kissed us goodnight. No one told us they loved us, and they'd see us in the morning," she wrote. "Sister Mary-Domenica shut off the lights and left. I started to cry."

Rosie told us that she lived for the kindness of strangers, including those who took her and some of the other kids out of the orphanage from time to time on day trips and to their homes for a holiday. She longed for any chance to be a regular girl. She told us what we knew to be true: It's the little things that mean the most.

Jason Wolfe, the founder of GiftCards.com and our 2015 honoree, also could have been one of the children served by our program. He grew up in an orphanage and told us that as a young boy, he wore the same worn jacket to school every day, even on the hottest days. Despite being teased and bullied, he never took it off. The reason? He wasn't wearing a shirt under it. He didn't own one.

When Jason was 10 and his mother could no longer take care of him, he wound up at the Milton Hershey School, a private boarding school for lower-income children. Jason loved his new school, and he wanted to grow up to be like the school's namesake—generous and caring toward others. When Jason was a young adult, a terrible accident left him with mounting medical bills. For a time he lived in his car. All the while, he was trying to get his business off the ground. Jason kept going. He didn't sell himself short. In Milton Hershey

----

2 Rosie Perez, *Handbook for an Unpredictable Life: How I Survived Sister Renata and My Crazy Mother, and Still Came Out Smiling (with Great Hair)*. (New York: Three Rivers Press, 2015).

style, Jason continues to give back and spread his kindness while teaching his young son to do the same.

Laura Schroff, co-author of the #1 *New York Times* bestseller *An Invisible Thread*, is another honoree who every day motivates me to do more and be better. Most important, she reminds me that one person can make a difference, and all it takes is kindness. Laura was a busy media executive who met an 11-year-old panhandler named Maurice on a walk on the Monday of Labor Day weekend. That day when Laura stopped, when Maurice asked for spare change for food, they began a miraculous relationship that changed both their lives forever.

Looking back at my own life, I am shocked at how one moment with one little girl impacted my life and helped so many of us make a difference. A newfound sense of gratitude and meditation practice contributed to the shift in my mindset as I got deeper and deeper into Pajama Program. I won't say it was easy, but I will tell you that you can do it, too. You are enough.

In the early days, when I didn't get what we needed for Pajama Program—and there were lots of days like that between the miracles—I started beating up on myself. I thought I wasn't qualified for what I was doing, that I was ridiculously unprepared for what I had taken on, that the "competition" was better than I was, and that I was a sad sack of an envoy for the children. Night after night, I twisted myself into a tight knot, tossing and turning until dawn.

My fears had to be kept at bay, and I learned to look for silver linings in my disappointments, which was not always easy. There was another shift that I struggled with greatly: letting go of the belief that there were "things" I not only wanted, but thought I needed.

When I was working in marketing, I was fulfilled because my hard work paid off and I could buy whatever I desired, go wherever I wanted, and carve out exactly the kind of life I'd always coveted. I know I wasn't alone in those thoughts. Climbing the corporate ladder, I met many women—and men—who shared my dreams and strategies for attaining every one of them.

We've all witnessed what I'm talking about—it's very common. It's extremely difficult to switch paths once we're on that road of "how much can I get for myself?" I began to see that the more I had, the more I wanted. All that "stuff" cluttered my mind as well as my physical space. I saw that I relied on these items to give meaning to my life. Those "things" had been my success markers; they were what made me happy and confident.

How would I be able to reconcile that loss? What would replace all the stuff I wanted if I couldn't have it? What would the absence of this stuff mean for my success, my hard work, and my self-esteem? These were daunting questions, and they forced me to rethink my priorities and, more important, my attitude.

I knew I had to make hard choices, and I was ashamed that I was making them at such a late stage in my life. I would have to let go of the desires I knew still lived deep in me—to fit in, and to look for success in status instead of purpose. But I never asked my *heart* how I wanted to live my life. I was on automatic like so many of us. That realization was part of what led me to Pajama Program.

When you let go of all the material things, you're forced to confront what you have inside of you, and as daunting as that can be, it's far more fulfilling in the long run than any shopping spree.

Why are we searching? What are we looking for? What do we need from life? If these questions go unanswered, we've been wandering aimlessly.

Our goal, really, is to find a place we feel we belong in this world. Isn't that what we all want? To belong somewhere? To matter to someone? My shift in mindset is something with which others grapple and can relate to. It's important to talk about this subject, dismantle it, and empower one another.

———

ALL THESE YEARS, I've carried around the image of that one little girl in my mind. The one who had never worn pajamas. She changed my life and the lives of so many others. I don't know her name. Maybe I don't remember it or maybe I never asked. I never had a photo of her from that late night, but what I remember most vividly are her eyes. They were big and round, and they drew me in like magnets. Strangely, I felt like I recognized her through her eyes. I was pulled to her, as if she knew me, and wanted me to understand something she couldn't tell me with her voice. What I saw was familiar. I felt like she wanted the same things I want, the same things we all want: love, acceptance, to be seen, that we matter in this world. There are so many more just like her waiting for us to find them.

One day recently, I was thinking about her and had an idea. I called my niece Nicole, a talented artist.

"If I describe that little girl to you exactly the way I remember her that night, could you sketch her for me?" I asked.

I described her in as much detail as possible. She wore a pink long-sleeve top with a lacy, flowered collar, purplish-pink pants that were too tight and too short, and dirty sneakers that were too big for her feet. Her blond pigtails were slightly lopsided. I also told Nicole that that little girl was somber all night, but when she stood in front of me, I thought I saw a glimmer in her eyes. Maybe I imagined it, but I could swear it was there.

I don't know the little girl's real name, but David, our cubicle donator, named her for me and it's perfect.

Her name is Hope. And there is enough of that, too.

Credit: Nicole Caggiano

The Heart of the Matter

* Lead with meaning.

WE ALL WANT to be seen and to know we make a difference. We need to feel respected and appreciated. Because when it comes right down to it, we're all in this together.

Make time to be still so your heart-voice can guide you. Believe in yourself and the power of one another. Then make the first move. Reach out. Connect. Share. Let go of regrets, forgive your mistakes, and rise again after disappointment. Leaders empower others to tell their stories. Lead with compassion; you will inspire others to do the same. And remember Hope. Our future depends upon it.

Find YOUR Pajamas

The Sky's the Limit

*M*any times in the past 20 years I've wondered how Pajama Program would get from Point A to Point B. Sometimes, the fear literally stopped me cold. In my toughest days, through daunting challenges and deepest doubts, I reminded myself of what held me to my purpose, and I offer these seven beliefs to you as you Find YOUR Pajamas.

1. I thought about another job and what that would be like. I decided to stay put, in my Pajamas.

2. On any day, I understood I was free to change my mind, do an about-face, or alter any direction. I made the decision every day to move forward, in my Pajamas.

3. Even if I didn't see the evidence every day, I chose to believe that working, in my Pajamas, was making a difference in the lives of unloved and frightened children.

4. I was responsible for my emotions. I could either succumb to stress or be still for peace of mind. I chose peace, in my Pajamas.

5. There were plenty of naysayers. I found my North Star and stood confidently, in my Pajamas.

6. I believed wholeheartedly that we had the partnership of the universe to support us, in our Pajamas.

7. I repeated my mantra: Feel the fear, and do it anyway, in my Pajamas.

———

WE'RE HERE TO make a difference. All it takes is one single second to react with kindness and to stop and make a compassionate gesture instead of hurrying on our way, same as usual. And when each of us connects to our purpose, the sky's the limit. There are more than enough miracles for all of us. No one's story is little. In this Pajama Program story, the children are little, but their stories are not. One person—*you*—can grow something big and summon the rest of us to help because there is enough. You are enough.

You can change the story of another life—and, in doing so, all of ours.

I wish you *Sweet Dreams*, in your Pajamas.

About the Author

*G*enevieve Piturro founded the hugely successful national non-profit Pajama Program when a six-year-old girl's question almost 20 years ago changed her life forever. After a career in television marketing, she jumped off the corporate ladder. Today, her Pajama Program has delivered seven million Good Nights filled with magical gifts of pajamas and books to children throughout the US.

Genevieve is now a professional speaker and consultant, sharing life and leadership lessons she learned through her Pajama Program journey. She has appeared on *The Oprah Winfrey Show, The Today Show, Good Morning America, The Early Show, CNN, and Fox & Friends* and has been featured in *O* magazine, *Forbes, The Wall Street Journal,* and *Parenting* magazine, among others. Genevieve has been the recipient of many awards, including the Shining World Compassion Award; SmartCEO Award of New York; Edith C. Macy Award for Distinguished Service (Westchester Children's Association); Friend of Abbott House Award; ANDRUS's Heart for Children's Award; and the Thomas J. Caramadre, Jr., Humanitarian Award. In November 2011, *914INC/Westchester Magazine* named Genevieve one of Westchester's Most Enterprising Women. Her story has been featured in several books, including *Angels on Earth: Inspiring Real-Life Stories of Fate, Friendship, and the Power of Kindness* by Laura Schroff and Alex Tresniowski and *Unselfish: Love Thy Neighbor as Thy Selfie* by Paul D. Parkinson.

Genevieve lives in Irvington, New York, with her husband Demo DiMartile (https://OneLightOneSpirit.com), who keeps her grounded and reaching for the stars!

For more information on Genevieve:
https://www.GenevievePiturro.com

For more information on Pajama Program:
https://www.PajamaProgram.org